UNDERSTANDING SPIRITUAL GROWTH
AND FRUIT BEARING

Got Fruit?

Darren Wilson

WESTBOW°
PRESS
A DIVISION OF THOMAS NELSON
& ZONDERVAN

All Scripture quotations in this publication are taken from
the King James Version of the Bible (KJV).

Scripture marked (AB) taken from the *Amplified Bible*, copyright © 1954, 1958, 1962, 1964, 1965, 1987 by The Lockman Foundation. Used by permission.

Scripture marked (NIV) taken from the Holy Bible, NEW INTERNATIONAL VERSION®. Copyright © 1973, 1978, 1984 by Biblica, Inc. All rights reserved worldwide. Used by permission. NEW INTERNATIONAL VERSION® and NIV® are registered trademarks of Biblica, Inc. Use of either trademark for the offering of goods or services requires the prior written consent of Biblica US, Inc.

Scripture marked (MSG) taken from The Message. Copyright © by Eugene H. Peterson 1993, 1994, 1995, 1996, 2000, 2001, 2002. Used by permission of NavPress Publishing Group.

Cover image by Cameron Hyman of Blue Skies Images
Author Photo by Elvis Harrigan of E. Harrigan Photography

WestBow Press books may be ordered through booksellers or by contacting:

WestBow Press
A Division of Thomas Nelson & Zondervan
1663 Liberty Drive
Bloomington, IN 47403
www.westbowpress.com
1 (866) 928-1240

ISBN: 978-1-4908-7973-4 (sc)
ISBN: 978-1-4908-7975-8 (hc)
ISBN: 978-1-4908-7974-1 (e)

Library of Congress Control Number: 2015907309

Print information available on the last page.

WestBow Press rev. date: 5/8/2015

Contents

Dedication

This book is dedicated to my grandmother, Effie Reid. Her unwavering commitment to instilling the Word of God in me from a young age, even during the times when I resisted her efforts, has resulted in this book—the first of many. Thank you for relentlessly taking the time to sow the incorruptible seed in my life back then; thank you for watering that seed, even now, with your prayers. That seed has taken root and begun to grow into a mighty tree of righteousness that the Lord has planted. Thank you for your obedience to Proverbs 22:6.

This book is also dedicated to my lovely wife, Charmaine Wilson. Our conversations and your love, support, and encouragement to write my convictions and thoughts down and your challenges have encouraged me to grow spiritually as a man, a husband, and eventually a father. Those talks and challenges inspired this first book. I am thankful and humbled that Almighty God saw fit to bless me with an amazing woman, one whose value far exceeds rubies. You truly are a lady of excellence. Thank you for your inspiration.

This book is also dedicated to my great grandchildren. This book was written on your behalf. Chances are I will be watching and cheering you on from the stands in heaven by the time you read this book. However, the principles in it will be just as relevant for your generation as for mine. May you use these principles to experience extraordinary growth and productivity as you fulfill your purpose during your journey on the earth.

I also dedicate this book to all those believers who desire a deeper, more fruitful and fulfilling relationship with God. May you discover the joy, fulfillment, and satisfaction of a fruitful and productive relationship with God through the pages of this book.

Ye have not chosen me, but I have chosen you and ordained you, that ye should go and bring forth fruit, and that your fruit should remain.

—John 15:16

Foreword

There is no more vital resource on one of the most significant subjects in the Bible. *Got Fruit* captures the importance of bearing fruit in the kingdom of God in a way that is lucid, yet challenging to religious concepts. From his introductory assertion to his final chapter, Darren Wilson has addressed a difficult topic and offered insight that is both relevant and revelatory.

At the heart of this book is a glorious vision of comprehensive transformation of individual lives. He says, with eloquence and clarity, "Growth is an indication that maturity is occurring. When maturity is occurring, fruit will begin to manifest itself in the lives of believers to the ultimate glory of God and His kingdom, of which we are a part."

This is significant because, beyond all the contradictions, complaints, and challenges, we must still bear fruit for kingdom impact in our societies. It's high time we do this. And we do not need even one more inspirational sermon or quick fix that appeases our flesh but does not change us from within. We must embrace strong truths that will bring us into compliance with God's eternal view on us.

After reading this manuscript, I predict that this book will do just that—propel us beyond our human stumbling and weaknesses and into the maturity necessary for kingdom purposes to be manifested on the earth through us. There is a clarion call to churches on every page: Grow up, mature, and express kingship in the world today.

Without reservation, it is my honor to recommend this book to every kingdom citizen who desires kingdom effectiveness. Please don't read it too quickly! Meditate on these potent truths by the spirit of wisdom and revelation. It's not necessarily a new message. However, it is one that will bring you into a place of transformation and enormous provision as a consequence of living by *Got Fruit?*

Brilliant work, Darren!

Dr. Alicia M. Liverpool
The David Company, Philipsburg, St. Maarten

Preface

Got Fruit? is my first book. It covers a very critical issue plaguing many born-again believers today. For as long as I can remember, I have been immersed in the Christian faith. My immediate family members are all Christians; my grandmother instilled the Word of God into my sister and me from a young age. I grew up in a church where I was always active in a variety of pursuits. I like to tell people that I was born in church because that phrase indicates how long I have been immersed in the culture of Christianity. However, as I grew older, I began to realize something. I noticed that many Christians who have been born again get stalled in an unproductive state and usually remain in that state until the day they pass from this life to the next.

I believe that this state of unproductiveness and barrenness is a direct result of little to no growth in many believers' lives and that it results in spiritual immaturity. Advances in science have clearly proven to us that all living things must grow to be effective. This is also the case with the spiritual self. If there is no spiritual growth, no indication that a believer's inner life is maturing, then it is safe to assume that there is no spiritual life within the believer. Such a person may be unproductive and have little to no influence on the environment with regard to the kingdom of God's affairs.

Jesus said it best in John 15:16: "Ye have not chosen me, but I have chosen you and ordained you, that ye should go and bring forth fruit, and that your fruit should remain." Jesus' point here was clear. He told His disciples that He chose them so He could help them grow to maturity and develop so that they might bear lasting fruit. When we are born again, therefore, Jesus' goal is to help us grow and develop so that we can bear fruit as an indication of that continuous growth process. I believe that the apparent lack of growth, maturity, development, and fruitfulness in citizens of the kingdom of God is the reason so many believers are frustrated with their lives. Their lack of growth hinders them from becoming all that they can be in the kingdom of God. In consequence, they exist in defeat, constantly hoping that their lives will get better. They do not realize that everything that they need to enjoy and get the most out of life has already been given to them. The only requirement is that they grow, mature, and develop in the faith to gain access to the abundant resources of the kingdom.

As an adult, I enjoy privileges that I could not have as a child because I was not mature enough to handle them. This same principle applies to spiritual matters. Only through spiritual growth and maturation can we enjoy the fullness of what the kingdom has to offer to us as citizens. My first book is my humble attempt at conveying the necessity for spiritual growth, maturity, and fruit bearing (productivity).

It is important that believers understand that spiritual maturation is imperative. It makes the difference between misery and fulfillment during our existence here on this earth. I wrote this book to help believers come to that realization.

Acknowledgments

For assistance with this book, which has taken me three years to prepare and one to write, I would like to acknowledge the following:

Pastor Emmanuel Carbon and the members of Christian Fellowship Church in St. Maarten—thank you for allowing me to walk in my gift by developing, refining, and experiencing many of these principles by sharing and practicing them with you.

Ambassador Alicia Liverpool and the David Company in St. Maarten—your unwavering commitment to the King and the increase of His kingdom as well as ensuring that He gets what He deserves has kept me motivated to complete this work and others that are in the pipeline. Thank you.

To all those I have not mentioned—life is rarely successful without the input, both positive and negative, of other individuals. This work is the product of the countless individuals whom I have had the privilege of encountering. Their ideas and perspectives have provided me with the knowledge, understanding, and wisdom that is recorded in this book.

Introduction

"Grow up!" We've all heard that command at some time. Growth is essential to life. Living beings were intentionally created and designed to grow and develop. Growth, therefore, is development or improvement toward a goal; and that goal is called maturity. The Word of God calls it "perfection" for the purpose of bearing fruit. When babies are born, they are immature physically and mentally, but we expect them to grow and develop. If they don't, there is a problem. When one initially becomes a believer, just as the baby is naturally immature, that person is spiritually immature. However, as time passes, the believer should develop and display the qualities or abilities (fruit) which, according to the Bible, characterize the mature and productive believer.

Many Scriptures describe the need to grow and mature spiritually.

Matthew 5:48 (AB): "You, therefore, must be perfect [growing into complete maturity of godliness in mind and character, having reached the proper height of virtue and integrity], as your heavenly Father is perfect."

Ephesians 4:14–15 (AB): So then, we may no longer be children, tossed [like ships] to and fro between chance gusts of teaching and wavering with every changing wind of doctrine, [the prey of] the cunning and cleverness of unscrupulous men, [gamblers engaged] in every shifting form of trickery in inventing errors to mislead." The theme of truth and maturation continues: "Rather, let our lives lovingly express truth [in all things, speaking truly, dealing truly, living truly]. Enfolded in love, let us grow up in every way and in all things into Him Who is the Head, [even] Christ (the Messiah, the Anointed One)."

Second Peter 3:18 (KJV) takes up the theme of growth: "But grow in grace, and in the knowledge of our Lord and Savior Jesus Christ. To him be glory both now and forever. Amen."

In 2 Thessalonians 1:3, we see that the Thessalonians grew exceedingly in faith: "We are bound to thank God always for you, brethren, as it is meet, because that your faith groweth exceedingly, and the charity of every one of you all toward each other aboundeth."

From the passages above, we can see that Scripture gives us clear indications that growth is expected of believers. For God, growth is not an option; it is a requirement. Many problems result when believers fail to grow. Some may go back to the ways of the world. Others cause strife in the church because of ignorance. Some harbor grudges and jealousy, while others become stumbling blocks because of irregular attendance, worldliness, or indifference. In the natural world, a baby needs to grow physically; in the spiritual arena, new believers need to grow spiritually.

The purpose of this book is to enlighten you, the reader, on the importance of both growing and bearing fruit and consequently spur you to do so.

Ask yourself the following questions.

→ What kind of spiritual growth have I experienced during the past months or years?

→ Is my mind being renewed?

→ Am I being productive?

→ Am I being fruitful?

I strongly believe that if we are serious about growing spiritually, becoming fruitful, and becoming productive, we should ask ourselves these questions at times. We must measure our progress because that's the only way we can know where we are in our journey to spiritual maturity. I use the word *journey* because spiritual maturity is not a destination. It is not a static location. As believers, every day we live is an opportunity to become more mature than we were the day before until that great day when our souls and bodies are finally redeemed.

If we do not take the time to develop and deepen our relationship with God, we are setting ourselves up for failure in this world, and God will hold us accountable for that. We all will stand before the judgment seat of Christ to give an account of everything we did (and didn't do) as it relates to His purpose on earth, as it is written in 2 Corinthians 5:10. This is not the time to straddle the fence of indecision. Right now, every believer has to be in a position to know God personally and intimately. Daniel wrote that "the people that know who God is will do great works for him" (Daniel 11:32). In the kingdom of God, there is more to see, hear, experience, and do than we can perceive. We must grow and mature in our faith to access it. This is not the time to live off yesterday's faith or past experiences. It's the time to develop your own walk with God and learn how to grow more deeply in God for yourself so that you may show Him to the world.

If you are reading this book, you are probably in search of such a path. You want to know God on a more personal and intimate level and wonder where to begin. I believe that this book will be a great asset to you. Parents and youth pastors, I believe that this book will be a great asset to you as well. It is important that you teach your children and your students, respectively, how vital it is to have a relationship with God and also how they can grow more deeply in that walk. I believe this book will equip you with the information and tools necessary to do so. Read the book. Write in it. Underline it. Use it as a study guide alongside the Bible and make sure what is in this book lines up with the inerrant Word of God. As you read, ask the Holy Spirit to speak to you and give you revelations concerning the different areas mentioned in this book. This book is meant as a valuable resource to anybody who wants to develop into a mature believer, able to withstand the changing winds of doctrine, and wants the same for others. I hope that this book will challenge you to enter into a deeper and more effective, productive and fruitful relationship with God.

Part I

The Nature and Process of Growth and Fruit Bearing

Chapter 1

Identity Crisis

On the Caribbean island of Saint Martin, where I was born and still live, there is an abundance of fruit trees. Sometimes there is fruit on the trees, and other times there is none, depending on the season. When there is no fruit on the trees, to know what fruit the tree produces, we usually ask, "What tree is this?"

That is a question of identity. We ask this question because knowing what kind of tree it is lets us know what fruit to expect. If you don't know the tree's identity, you have no idea what fruit will be produced. So, before we begin to talk about growth and fruit bearing, we must discuss the concept of identity.

What is identity?

Etymology is the study of the origin of words, and the online etymology dictionary[1] reveals that the root word for *identity* comes from the Latin word *idem,* which means *the same.* So identity literally

---

[1] http://www.etymonline.com/index.php?term=identity&allowed_in_frame=0

means *sameness* or *oneness*, but not in the sense of uniformity. Your identity comes from being the "same as something" or "one with something" in the context of moral, ethical, intellectual, and/or cultural characteristics—in other words, the same in nature. An identity comes from the fact that a person or entity is the same in essential nature as another person or entity.

Allow me to use myself as an illustration of this concept. I am from the island of Saint Martin and therefore my demonym is Saint Martiner. What is interesting about that is I do not *look* like every other Saint Martiner nor does every other Saint Martiner *look* like me. Saint Martiners do not have a uniformed appearance however, as Saint Martiners, we are all *one* because we have things in common and we share the same culture and nature. One identifier of our nature and culture is our accent with certain colloquial slangs and idioms. All Saint Martiners have an accent that identifies us. The same applies to persons from Anguilla, St. Kitts, Dominica, St. Lucia, Grenada, and Trinidad. These islands all have persons that do not look alike but they have something in common that identifies them which is their accent and that accent reveals a part of their nature and identity.

This illustration is corroborated in the following two biblical passages:

> There is neither Jew nor Greek, there is neither bond nor free, there is neither male nor female: for ye are all one in Christ Jesus.
>
> —Galatians 3:28

> For as the body is one, and hath many members, and
> all the members of that one body, being many, are
> one body: so also is Christ. For by one Spirit are we
> all baptized into one body, whether we be Jews or
> Gentiles, whether we be bond or free; and have been
> all made to drink into one Spirit.
> —1 Corinthians 12:12-13

Just to re-iterate, I do not look like every other Saint Martiner and neither does every other Saint Martiner look like me. What identifies us despite the fact that we do not look alike is the reality that we are all called Saint Martiners because being a Saint Martiner bears a certain kind of fruit (culture) that is evidenced in us. Likewise, in the passages listed above we see very clearly that although all believers may not necessarily look alike (Jews or Greeks, bond or free, male or female), they all find their *identity* in Jesus Christ and that identification also bears a certain kind of fruit which we will explore in further detail later in the book.

Now the word *identity* is not found anywhere in Scripture, so we can't look for that word to study it as such. The concept of identity is there, and since we have the root meanings of the word, we can look that up in Scripture. Remember, the root of the word *identity* carries the ideas of *commonality, solidarity, or oneness* therefore we have to see what the Word has to say about these terms as it relates to us.

The Word says that we, as believers, are identified with—have the same nature as—Christ (Colossians 2:13 and 3:3; Galatians 2:20). We are identified with—have the same nature as—Christ by being *in* Him (John 15:1–5; Romans 6:1–4). The results of being identified with Christ are as follows.

- We are new creations (2 Corinthians 5:17).
- We have wisdom, righteousness, sanctification, and redemption (1 Corinthians 1:30).
- We have peace (Romans 5:1).

That is what the Word of God means in John 1:16, when the apostle writes that we have received of His fullness, and in Colossians 2:9–10, where it is written that we are made complete or full in Him. As a result of that new nature, we are now enabled to emulate the standard mentioned in 1 John 4:17: "as He is, so are we in this world."

Types and Shadows

When we begin to study the Bible, especially the Old Testament, we see it is riddled with examples of what are called "types and shadows." What are types and shadows? In the following passages, we see these two words used. In Romans 5:14, Paul writes to the Roman believers: "Nevertheless death reigned from Adam to Moses, even over them that had not sinned after the similitude of Adam's transgression, who is the figure of him that was to come." *The Amplified Bible* uses the term *type* instead of *figure* to refer to the same concept.

The writer of Hebrews uses the term *shadow* instead.

> Who serve unto the example and shadow of heavenly
> things, as Moses was admonished of God when he

was about to make the tabernacle: for, See, saith he, that thou make all things according to the pattern shewed to thee in the mount.

—Hebrews 8:5

For the law having a shadow of good things to come, and not the very image of the things, can never with those sacrifices which they offered year by year continually make the comers thereunto perfect.

—Hebrews 10:1

In the passage from the letter to the Romans, *figure* is also translated as *type*. In the Greek of the New Testament, *figure* is *Tupos* (Strong G5179), which means "a person or thing prefiguring a future (Messianic) person or thing." In the passage in the letter to the Hebrews, *shadow* is translated from the Greek as *skia* (Strong G4639), which means "an image cast by an object and representing the form of that object."

Types and shadows, in a very basic sense, are physical realities used as examples to make spiritual truths more comprehensible. For example, one of the most well-known types and shadows is that of the Passover lamb in Exodus, which is a type of Jesus Christ and a shadow of the atonement Jesus accomplished for us on the cross at Calvary.

Using this concept of types and shadows, it is clear that the usage of spiritual fruit in Scripture denotes a correlation to physical fruit. In terms of spiritual growth and productivity in a believer's life, the Word almost always makes mention of fruit. Why fruit? Fruit is an indication of growth and productivity, and just as fruit needs time to grow, these qualities require time to grow in the life of the believer and community.

Vine, Branches, and Fruit

In John 15:1–7, Jesus continues teaching the disciples, using the type and shadow example in which He is the "true Vine" and His followers are the "branches."

> I am the true vine, and my Father is the husbandman. Every branch in me that beareth not fruit he taketh away: and every branch that beareth fruit, he purgeth it, that it may bring forth more fruit. Now ye are clean through the word which I have spoken unto you. Abide in me, and I in you. As the branch cannot bear fruit of itself, except it abide in the vine; no more can ye, except ye abide in me. I am the vine, ye are the branches: He that abideth in me, and I in him, the same bringeth forth much fruit: for without me ye can do nothing. If a man abide not in me, he is cast forth as a branch, and is withered; and men gather them, and cast them into the fire, and they are burned. If ye abide in me, and my words abide in you, ye shall ask what ye will, and it shall be done unto you.

The true vine, Jesus, is likely comparing Himself to a grapevine, which has branches stemming from the vine. The branches only produce fruit if they are attached to, or identified with, the vine. The implication here is that Jesus, as the Vine, is the center of the

Christian faith. He is the source of life and the way to eternal life. Every person who is born again by the Spirit is now a spiritual branch grafted onto the true Vine by faith (Romans 11:11–24). As a result, the branches are able to produce fruit because they have the same nature and qualities the vine has.

In other words, this is what happened.

The day you were born again, you received Jesus' identity by faith and joined with Him. When that happened, your sinfulness was exchanged for His righteousness. Now, whenever the Father looks at you, He sees you through the person of His righteous Son, Jesus. Because Jesus is righteous and has become your identity, the Father sees you with a righteous identity too (2 Corinthians 5:21; Romans 3:22). Because of your newfound righteousness by faith in the completed work of Jesus, you are now a cleansed vessel, purged through the blood of Jesus, because everything is made clean through the blood, and without bloodshed, there is no remittance of sin (Hebrews 9:22). The Holy Spirit of God can now take up residence in you. So when God's Spirit moves into your spirit and becomes one with your spirit, everything that is in God now becomes part of you. You now have unlimited access to everything God has promised in Ephesians 1:3 because all His promises in Jesus—to us—are affirmed, as written in 2 Corinthians 1:20.

Branches are more productive when pruned. The *Merriam-Webster Dictionary and Thesaurus* defines pruning as follows:

- V. To cut off unwanted parts (as of a tree)

Using these definitions in the context of this Scripture, the pruning process may refer to

1) the painful cutting away through adversity and difficulty, which ultimately produces faithfulness and a closer relationship with God; or

2) the extrication of dead branches, which would mean the pruning entails removing what is undesirable and hinders the effective production of fruit.

Sometimes the part about unproductive branches being taken away is interpreted as the believer losing his or her salvation. Let me interject here that this refers to the believer growing in the faith and bearing fruit as evidence of that growth—not the believer's salvation. Once a person has indicated and professed faith in Jesus Christ and His finished work in a public setting, evidenced by water baptism and the infilling of the Holy Ghost, his or her salvation is secured. However, whether they grow and begin to show fruit from that initial point of salvation is another issue. That is what Jesus was alluding to in this final discourse with His followers.

Jesus gave us the key to bearing fruit in John 15:7. He said His words need to abide in us. If not, we cannot bear fruit and will be cut off. Then we cannot be used to bear fruit so others may benefit from and taste and see the Lord is good, as written in Psalm 34:8, through us. This concept also applies to churches. If a church is not attached to the Vine, it will not bear fruit. If a church is not committed to producing fruit, it will be cut off spiritually. God will not use it to affect change in the earth on His behalf because the church is not abiding in His words. The church that is spiritually cut off from producing fruit will have to be grafted back into the Vine to produce fruit, as written in Romans 11:11–24 and it is grafted back in by returning to His Word.

Fruit is a manifestation of whatever is in you.

One incontrovertible fact about knowing the identity of a tree is that you know what kind of fruit it will produce. Jesus explained this fact very clearly in Matthew 7:17–20: "Even so every good tree bringeth forth good fruit; but a corrupt tree bringeth forth evil fruit. A good tree cannot bring forth evil fruit, neither can a corrupt tree bring forth good fruit. Every tree that bringeth not forth good fruit is hewn down, and cast into the fire. Wherefore by their fruits ye shall know them."

Fruit bearing is linked to identity. For example, if we can identify a tree as a mango tree, we know that tree will only produce mangoes. A mango tree cannot bear avocados because its nature is to produce mangoes. James, the brother of Jesus, alluded to this fact in James 3:12 when he asked, "Can the fig tree, my brethren, bear olive berries? either a vine, figs?"

Unless we know the identity or nature of the tree, we cannot know what fruit it will produce. The same principle applies spiritually. If you want to bear spiritual fruit, there must be a spiritual identity or nature. A spiritual identity can only be achieved by being born again of the Spirit, which Jesus clearly outlined in John 3:3–6.

Jesus answered and said unto him, Verily, verily, I say unto thee, Except a man be born again, he cannot see the kingdom of God.

Nicodemus saith unto him, How can a man be born when he is old? can he enter the second time into his mother's womb, and be born? Jesus answered, Verily, verily, I say unto thee, Except a man be born of water and of the Spirit, he cannot enter into the kingdom of God. That which is born of the flesh is flesh; and that which is born of the Spirit is spirit.

People who are born-again Christians automatically have all that is necessary to produce spiritual fruit because they are connected to the spiritual vine which is Jesus Christ, as it is written in 2 Peter 1:2–4.

Grace and peace be multiplied unto you through the knowledge of God, and of Jesus our Lord, According as his divine power hath given unto us all things that pertain unto life and godliness, through the knowledge of him that hath called us to glory and virtue: Whereby are given unto us exceeding great and precious promises: that by these ye might be partakers of the divine nature, having escaped the corruption that is in the world through lust.

So, for kingdom citizens, born-again believers in the Lord Jesus Christ, our identities are linked to the fact that we are connected to Jesus Christ and therefore belong to a new order. That order produces a new culture or fruit: a new category of people called kingdom citizens. Culture, in this context, is another way of saying *the fruit of a people* because people are identified by their culture. We are identified by our new nature, which produces a new culture, not by a title. We are identified solely by the cultural identity of the kingdom, which is the fruit of the Spirit, which we will look at in the next chapter.

Chapter 2

The Fruit of the Spirit

Several years ago I had the opportunity to preach my first message surrounding the topic of the fruit of the Spirit at church. While I was preparing to preach, I was very focused on extracting a profound message from the different elements; I hoped for divine revelation or insight into the hidden meaning of love, joy, and peace. I can just imagine Jesus and Paul having a good laugh over that effort. During my study, I felt impelled to pay more attention to the beginning and the end of the text because only then would the middle make sense. Now, with the help of the Holy Spirit, I will attempt to very briefly summarize the entire passage.

Paul's passage on the fruit of the spirit, in his letter to the Galatians, is very familiar. He lists some virtues that make up the fruit of the Spirit.

> But the fruit of the Spirit is love, joy, peace, longsuffering, gentleness, goodness, faith, meekness, temperance: against such there is no law.

Before continuing, I would like to emphasize some points within this important text, Galatians 5:22–23. Please note the words *fruit* and *Spirit* and all the virtues of the fruit, beginning at *love* and ending with *temperance.*

It is interesting to note that the passage begins, "But the fruit (singular) of the Spirit." However, there is more than one virtue listed. One thing I have noticed is that it is often the simplest and most clear observations that confuse us the most. Why is the singular form of the word *fruit* used? I believe the Bible was divinely inspired, which means that God didn't make a grammatical error in this particular passage.

So why would this be important? Well, let us use, as an example, a fruit tree that everyone is familiar with: the apple tree. The apple tree can only produce one type of fruit, apples. Now while an apple tree can have many branches, some branches may bear more apples than others. Nevertheless, they all produce the same type of fruit.

Although there are nine virtues, they all make up one fruit. This means that these nine virtues form a whole spiritual fruit, which I do not view as coincidental. God, in all His wisdom, knew that we would adopt a grocery store mentality regarding the application of the fruit of the Spirit. This means that we would pick and choose the elements that we want and leave the ones that we do not want, as we do at the grocery store. That mindset would not be what He intended. To prevent that mindset from spreading, God, being proactive, inspired the apostle Paul to use the singular form of the word *fruit* to illustrate that point.

For example, just as it is not possible to get the core of the apple without first taking apart the whole fruit, it is not possible to say, "Well I'm going just take self-control and not gentleness," or "I'm going to have faith but leave meekness alone until a later date." There are different parts to an apple, but they all come together to make one fruit.

Friends, this is a package deal—nine different virtues, but one whole fruit. A mango tree cannot produce mangos without skin, nor can an avocado tree produce avocados without the edible flesh. Likewise, a person cannot claim to bear fruit as a growing and maturing believer while consistently demonstrating deficiency in love, temperance, or gentleness; fruit does not work like that.

In Galatians 5:16, Paul mentions that believers should endeavor to "walk in the Spirit" so as not to give in to the lust of the flesh. Maintaining that context, we can infer that the phrase "fruit of the Spirit" in verse 22 is most likely referring to fruit that the Spirit-led life produces and presents a list of the desires and characteristics God cultivates in believers through His Spirit. This list describes believers who are led by the Spirit and who are directed by God's dynamic presence and awesome grace at work in their lives, not the dictates of the law. I did some research on these nine virtues and found some of this information very enlightening, so let us go through the list for a basic understanding of these nine virtues.

Nine Virtues of the Fruit of the Spirit

Love

It is only fitting to start with love. Once again, it is no coincidence that love is the first item on the list. Love is mentioned first because, as born-again believers, we should make love the basis for everything that we do. That is exactly what Jesus commanded us to do. The Greek word for love is *agape* (Strong G26) and means *unconditional love*. My definition of unconditional love is "love that is not dependent on external circumstances but solely to show genuine concern for others regardless of how they treat you or how you feel."

Love is probably one of the most used and most misunderstood words in the English language. Nowadays we use *love* to refer to anything or anyone we enjoy or like. However, this is not the way that God intended for us to love. The most famous and often quoted passage about love is found in the Apostle Paul's first letter to the Corinthian church. Here is what it says:

> Love is patient, love is kind. It does not envy, it does not boast, it is not proud. It does not dishonor others, it is not self-seeking, it is not easily angered, it keeps no record of wrongs. Love does not delight in evil but rejoices with the truth. It always protects, always trusts, always hopes, always perseveres. Love never fails.
> —1 Corinthians 13:4–8 (NIV)

The reason Paul gave a detailed description of love to the Corinthian believers was due to their detrimental deficiency in love. Careful observation from the text reveals that, first and foremost, love is patient and kind. I believe that, as born-again believers, we may become so overwhelmed with incorporating all Paul's attributes of love that we give up before we even start. However, if we would concentrate on cultivating patience and kindness, the other eight attributes would be less challenging. Patience and kindness stand in opposition to envy, conceit, pride, dishonor, selfishness, irascibility, resentment, and immorality. Paul's last four positive descriptors express attitudes that a person who is exhibiting genuine *agape* will demonstrate. All these attributes are to be displayed in an unbiased manner towards others to display God's *agape* love for humanity through us.

Joy

We often use *joy* and *happiness* interchangeably, but joy does not necessarily equate to happiness. In Greek, *joy* is *chara* (G5479). Here is a quote from Rick Renner, author of *Sparkling Gems from the Greek*, to shed more light on this word:

> The Greek word for 'joy' is chara, derived from the word charis, which is the Greek word for 'grace'. This is significant to note, for chara is produced by the charis of God. This means 'joy' is not a human-based happiness that comes and goes but, rather, true 'joy' is divine in its origin. It is a Spirit-given expression that flourishes best in hard times.

Therefore, the difference between joy and happiness is that joy comes from God and is not dependent on external circumstances. Joy is an internal state. Happiness is an emotion and depends on current, external conditions. That is why when a woman gives birth it is called the "joy of childbirth," not the "happiness of childbirth." There is nothing happy about the pain of the birthing process. However, there is joy in the satisfaction of knowing that there will be a healthy baby to love, nurture, and help to develop and fulfill his or her purpose. We find this kind of joy mentioned in Hebrews 12:2:

"Looking unto Jesus the author and finisher of our faith; who for the joy that was set before him endured the cross, despising the shame, and is set down at the right hand of the throne of God."

There was nothing happy about the pain, suffering, and shame that Jesus endured during the crucifixion process. However there was joy in knowing that at the end of the process, the sins of the whole world would be removed, and salvation made available to all, for the purposes of His kingdom's advancement.

Peace

In my final year of high school, encouraged by my English teacher, I entered a speech competition. I wrote and delivered a speech on world peace, and I remember that my definition of *peace* at that time was "a state of calmness or quietness." The Greek word for peace is *eirene* (Strong G1515), and it also has similar meanings such as *being one or whole, quietness, or rest.* Its Greek root is *eiro,* which means *to join.* So *eirene* means *to join together to make complete, one, or whole.* Rick Renner, author of *Sparkling Gems from the Greek,* describes the Greek word for peace eloquently.

> The word "peace" comes from the Greek word eirene, the Greek equivalent for the Hebrew word shalom, which expresses the idea of wholeness, completeness, or tranquility in the soul that is unaffected by the outward circumstances or pressures. The word eirene strongly suggests the rule of order in place of chaos. When a person is dominated by peace, he has a calm, inner stability that results in the ability to conduct

himself peacefully, even in the midst of circumstances that would normally be very nerve-wracking, traumatic, or upsetting … Rather than allowing the difficulties and pressures of life to break him, a person who is possessed by peace is whole, complete, orderly, stable, and poised for blessing.

Peace is evidence of a state of wholeness or completeness in the spiritual, emotional, and physical areas in an individual's life. Peace comes as a result of seeking after God; that is the only way one can get true peace. Isaiah 26:3 describes such peace: "Thou wilt keep him in perfect peace, whose mind is stayed on thee: because he trusteth in thee."

So, is peace (wholeness or completeness in every area of life) the direct result of complete trust or faith in God and your relationship with Him? In Psalm 29:11 the psalmist writes, "The Lord will give strength unto his people; the Lord will bless his people with peace."

Despite what may be going on around you, you may still experience an innate sense of wholeness that transcends natural logic because it is a peace that only God can provide. As an anonymous author wrote, "Peace is not the absence of conflict; it is the presence of God, no matter what the conflict."

Longsuffering

The Greek word for *longsuffering* used here is a compound word, *makrothumia* (Strong 3115), or *makrothumos* (Strong 3116), which can be translated as either *patience* or *endurance*. For precision, the noun form will be treated as a compound in this book. The compound word is made of two words, *macros* (Strong 3117) and *thumos* (Strong 2372) which mean "long or long lasting" and "passion or anger" respectively. We can interpret the meaning as "the ability to keep your anger under control for a long time, usually while enduring bad behavior from others." An example of this word in this context is found in Acts 26:1–3. Paul was defending himself in the presence of King Agrippa.

> Then Agrippa said unto Paul, Thou art permitted to speak for thyself. Then Paul stretched forth the hand, and answered for himself: I think myself happy, king Agrippa, because I shall answer for myself this day before thee touching all the things whereof I am accused of the Jews: Especially because I know thee to be expert in all customs and questions which are among the Jews: wherefore I beseech thee to hear me patiently.
>
> —Acts 26:1–3

In the third verse, Paul requested that King Agrippa bear patiently *(makrothumos)* with his detailed defense against the Jews' accusations against him without becoming agitated, annoyed, or angry. In this practical application, *longsuffering* refers to keeping one's temper when annoyed.

In situations where longsuffering is needed, we can help ourselves by remembering that God Himself was just as longsuffering with humanity with regard to salvation. For about four thousand years, God exhibited longsuffering with depraved humanity before revealing

Himself in the form of Jesus Christ. Even so, He is still "reserving His anger for the day of judgment," as it is written in Romans 2:5. Still, that extended endurance is an example of His longsuffering with humanity. On a more personal level, however long it took you to become born again is an example of God's longsuffering toward you. His longsuffering and forbearance in the form of His goodness to you led you to repentance, as it is articulated in Romans 2:4. How long, therefore, should we extend the same tolerance to others? Also important to note is that this same idea of longsuffering applies to us as well. Sometimes we need to show more longsuffering to ourselves than we need to show others.

Gentleness

The Greek word *chrestos* (Strong 5543) means *kind* or *pleasant*. Kindness is acting for the good of everybody even when they don't deserve it. When we think of pleasantness, we think of an attitude that is not harsh or bitter. Bitterness, harshness, and hostility alienate people and make them feel that there is no room for honest mistakes. For example, if we are correcting someone, pleasantness makes our correction more acceptable and the person more receptive.

Goodness

Agathosune (Strong 19) means "uprightness in heart and life," which we can interpret as *good*. First there must be a standard to measure "uprightness in heart and life," and Jesus, in Mark 10:18, gave us that standard: "And Jesus said unto him, Why callest thou me good? there is none good but one, that is, God."

In this verse we see Jesus clarifying that God is the standard by which we should measure goodness because He is the only one who is good. So if God is the standard by which we measure our goodness, that means we have to look to God's Word, since God and His Word are one, as written in John 1:1. We are to use that standard to determine if we are "upright in heart and life." A good person acts in ways consistent with correct beliefs, politeness, obedience, and moral excellence according to the Word. This standard for goodness is very clear. Goodness involves right action at the right time, all the time, even when it is unpopular. This speaks of an individual's character and indicates that the person can be trusted to act with integrity and moral excellence.

Faith

We get our word *faith* from the Greek *pistis* (Strong 4102), which means *belief* or *conviction*. It derives from *pethio* (Strong 3982), *to persuade through words*. The implication here is this: What an individual is persuaded to believe is directly related to what that person hears. It is no small wonder, then, that Paul wrote in Romans 10:17: "So then faith cometh by hearing, and hearing by the word of God."

Faith is therefore developed by a continuous display of total belief and trust in God. Believers allow Him to strengthen their conviction and belief through constant persuasion by the use of His Word. So when we believe, we are convinced and persuaded that God will do what He promised in His Word; that is faith.

The apostle James elaborated upon the connection between faith and works.

> What doth it profit, my brethren, though a man say
> he hath faith, and have not works? can faith save him?
> If a brother or sister be naked, and destitute of daily
> food, And one of you say unto them, Depart in peace,
> be ye warmed and filled; notwithstanding ye give
> them not those things which are needful to the body;
> what doth it profit? Even so faith, if it hath not works,
> is dead, being alone. Yea, a man may say, Thou hast
> faith, and I have works: shew me thy faith without thy
> works, and I will shew thee my faith by my works.
>
> —James 2:14–18

James wrote that faith without works is dead. Now *works* not only means healings and miracles here, though those are two valid works. James meant that faith must be backed up by everyday actions. If you say you believe in God but your actions don't convey the same message, your faith is unsupported and ineffectual. Faith does not only believe; faith acts, and the faithful are not hearers only of the Word but doers as well, as stated in James 1:22. You can only do what you hear when you are convinced that what you heard is the truth. Genuine faith motivates corresponding action.

Meekness

Meekness has been misinterpreted as weakness. Meekness, which comes from the Greek *praotes* (Strong 4236), is similar to gentleness. Meekness is humble gentleness. The root word of *praotes* is *praus* (Strong 4239), meaning "mildness of disposition, gentleness of spirit, meekness. Meekness toward God is that disposition of spirit in which we accept His dealings with us as good, and therefore without disputing or resisting."

This describes an attitude of humility, a realization that God is in control and we are not. God says, in Proverbs 16:5, that proud people are an abomination to Him. Being proud really is asking God, "Who are You?" and claiming, "I don't need You. I only need me, myself and I." That is a recipe for disaster, as specified in Proverbs 16:18—"Pride goeth before destruction, and an haughty spirit before a fall."

God never supports proud people because pride is making yourself your own God. When you set yourself up as your own God, then you are assuming responsibility for yourself. Therefore, a proud person cannot receive any help from God because he thinks that he does not need the help in the first place. James 4:6 expresses God's response to pride—"But he giveth more grace. Wherefore he saith, God resisteth the proud, but giveth grace unto the humble."

Pride got Satan kicked out of heaven. When that happened, he came to Adam and was able to influence him and got Adam expelled from his rightful environment, the Garden of Eden, as well. Ever since then, Satan has been trying to kick humanity out of our rightful kingdom environment. He does this by influencing humans with pride so that they, too, can fall under the same condemnation that got him banished. However, with the virtue of meekness, we are able to overcome that prideful tendency.

Temperance

I believe that temperance is the most straightforward characteristic on this list, and yet it is the most difficult to attain. People generally want to indulge without restraint and have a serious problem when prohibited from doing so. In addition to that, the "If it feels good, do it" sensual mentality of the world is not helping the situation either. Almost everywhere in the world, we are bombarded with images promoting human cultures that lack temperance.

The Greek word for temperance is *egkrateia,* which means self-control—the virtue of one who masters his desires and passions, especially his sensual appetites. A temperate person has control over appetites and desires and can resist the immense temptations to indulgence. The apostle Paul reminded the Corinthian church of the necessity of self-control.

> And every man that striveth for the mastery is temperate in all things. Now they do it to obtain a corruptible crown; but we an incorruptible. I therefore so run, not as uncertainly; so fight I, not as one that beateth the air: But I keep under my body, and bring it into subjection: lest that by any means, when I have preached to others, I myself should be a castaway.
>
> —1 Corinthians 9:25–27

Much like contemporary athletes, Greek athletes underwent strict, vigorous training to be the best. They often abstained from unhealthy food, alcohol, and sex because these interfered with their ability to perform at the highest level possible. Paul is drawing the analogy between athletes and the life of a believer by saying that if athletes can learn and understand the importance of self-control to be the best at their athletic endeavors, so too born-again believers can learn and understand the importance of self-control to be effective kingdom citizens. Also important to note is Paul's emphasis on self-control, not control of other people. This leaves no margin for immature behavior and blaming others when we don't meet our goals.

As stated earlier, there are nine virtues that make up the whole fruit of the Spirit. The nine can be divided evenly into three groups of three. This is significant to me because a fruit consists of different parts but is still one fruit. The same principle applies to the Spirit. If we refer once again to nature, we observe that an apple has three parts—the core, the edible flesh, and the skin. Along the same lines, from the spiritual aspect, the fruit of the Spirit has three parts: the core (love, joy, peace), the flesh (longsuffering, gentleness, goodness), and the skin (faith, meekness, temperance).

The core is the inner part of the apple. It holds the life of the apple and the life to produce more apples, which are the seeds. The first three virtues of the fruit of the Spirit are the core of the fruit of the Spirit. Love, joy, and peace are cultivated in the believer's inner life to produce the other the six virtues. When we have the love of God, the joy of the Lord, and the peace of God working within us, we will begin to think and act differently.

The next part of the apple is the flesh, the nutritious part we can eat. When we eat the flesh, its nutrients nourish us. The next three virtues are like that part of the avocado we eat. Longsuffering, gentleness, and goodness appeal to our fellow men because those virtues nourish them. When other people see these virtues in us, they also see the power of the Spirit alive in us and working through us. Its power allows us to behave differently from everybody else. Our example nourishes others from within to bring about change in their lives.

Last is the skin of the apple. The skin protects the fruit from outside infections and absorbs impacts to keep the core, seed, and flesh safe. Faith, meekness, and temperance are like the skin of the Spirit's fruit. These help protect the core from unbelief, pride, anger, lust, and other negative tendencies. Faith, meekness and temperance, as quiet as they sound, are actually the ones fighting against our flesh. Every day we are faced with situations and decisions that can make us doubt God, become proud, or lose our tempers. If the skin is destroyed before the fruit is ripe, then the whole fruit is destroyed because its protection is no longer there.

In all my long observation of fruit trees, I have never seen a fruit grow its core, flesh, and skin separately. It is not possible. That is why I emphasize that the Spirit's fruit is a package deal; you can't have one part without the others. If you go through all the virtues again, you will observe that they are interrelated; that is why it is *fruit* singular. Just as the natural fruit's core, flesh, and skin grow together to produce one edible, mature fruit, so each group or each virtue grows together to produce one nourishing and mature spiritual fruit.

Chapter 3

Different Kinds of Fruit

The fruit of the Spirit is not the only fruit that a Spirit-led life produces. One of the definitions of *fruit* from the *Merriam-Webster Dictionary and Thesaurus* is "the effect or consequence of an action or operation" as in "The pupils began to appreciate the fruit of their labors." This leads us to ascertain that spiritual fruit is not limited to the fruit of the Spirit; it is any manifestation or production resulting from the work of a Spirit-led life. The fruit of the tree manifests the tree's work.

In *Releasing Your Potential,* best-selling author Dr. Myles Munroe defined work as simply "to become." In work, a person becomes what he was created to be, and if that is happening, that person's fruitful manifestations should be evident. Here are some verses in the gospel of John in which Jesus spoke about work.

> Jesus said to them, My food (nourishment) is to do the will (pleasure) of Him Who sent Me and to accomplish and completely finish His work.
>
> —John 4:34 (AB)

But Jesus answered them, My Father has worked [even] until now, [He has never ceased working; He is still working] and I, too, must be at [divine] work.

—John 5:17 (AB)

For the Father loveth the Son, and sheweth him all things that himself doeth: and he will shew him greater works than these, that ye may marvel.

—John 5:20 (KJV)

But I have as My witness something greater (weightier, higher, better) than that of John; for the works that the Father has appointed Me to accomplish and finish, the very same works that I am now doing, are a witness and proof that the Father has sent Me.

—John 5:36 (AB)

Jesus answered, It was not that this man or his parents sinned, but he was born blind in order that the workings of God should be manifested (displayed and illustrated) in him. We must work the works of Him Who sent Me and be busy with His business while it is daylight; night is coming on, when no man can work.

—John 9:3–4 (AB)

Verily, verily, I say unto you, He that believeth on me, the works that I do shall he do also; and greater works than these shall he do; because I go unto my Father.

—John 14:12 (KJV)

Here Jesus spoke of work that results in fruitful spiritual manifestations, works validating the message of the kingdom that He preached. These manifestations included miracles, healings, deliverances, authoritative teachings, and others. Here are a few of the points I gathered from these verses on this subject of work:

1) *To work* essentially means *to produce, to cause to exist, to become productive.* Work was created by God and is therefore good. Work is also meant to glorify God, who gave you the work to do.

2) God, being the first worker, became productive and caused the universe and the world to exist, producing all that we see. So when we engage in legitimate forms of work, we are performing a God-ordained activity.

3) God's work also glorifies Him, and *glorify* means "to give an accurate representation of" or "to reveal the full nature of" or "to show off." So when we engage in authentic forms work, we represent and reveal the full nature of God.

4) God made everything to work (produce). Plants produce oxygen, trees produce fruit, and soil produces minerals and precious stones. When God created Adam, He placed him in the garden and told him to work (produce) too by tilling the ground and naming the animals and other creations.

Therefore, if we have been stamped with a "made in God's image" stamp and are not engaging in legitimate work and productivity, we are not fulfilling our purpose. We are also not being proper and accurate representatives of a God who is productive and favors productivity.

Working is producing what you were created and designed to produce. Ephesians 2:10 puts it this way: "For we are his workmanship, created in Christ Jesus unto good works, which God hath before ordained that we should walk in them."

So if we want to see a generation of entrepreneurs, doctors, lawyers, government officials, educators, advisors, lawmakers, economists, writers, singers, musicians, music producers, actors, architects, engineers, contractors, IT specialists, fashion designers, athletes, tradesmen and women who will alert the world to the kingdom of heaven for the glory of God, we have to become productive via fruitful manifestations of the Spirit in all these areas.

God's glory is simply the nature and character of God on display. When you are doing what God gifted and graced you to do, you give God glory. Jesus said, in Matthew 5:16, "Let your light so shine before men that they may see your good works and glorify your Father which is in heaven."

What are these good works? They are the good works prepared for you to do before the foundation of the world, as we saw earlier in Ephesians 2:10. Your light is your gifts and talents. Fruit is the manifestation of the good works prepared for you to do in fulfillment of God's purpose for you. His purpose is based on the gifts and talents God gave you for use in your generation. If you are gifted in any area, God expects you to use those gifts to be fruitful.

Since we all have good works that were created for us to do before the beginning of the world, God will confirm those good works via manifestations of the Spirit. This is also known as fruit. If you are meant to teach, you will manifest your fruit through a high level of knowledge and wisdom. If you are meant to evangelize, multiple salvations will be manifested in your life. If your purpose is in deliverance, then discerning of spirits and/or exorcism is the fruit that will be manifested in your life. If your purpose is in business, then administrative, organizational, and economic occupations will be the fruit manifested in your life. If your purpose is in the arts, then expression through creative ability is your fruit.

The *Amplified Bible* version of Ecclesiastes 9:10 has advice on commitment to work. "Whatever your hand finds to do, do it with all your might, for there is no work or device or knowledge or wisdom in Sheol (the place of the dead), where you are going."

Jesus echoed this verse in John 9:4 when He spoke about working while it was day. Whatever your hand finds to do (whatever you are gifted and graced to do), do it with all your might (do it with the grace that God has given you to complete your good works and be fruitful); and do so while it is day (while you are still alive) because night is approaching, and then no man can work (when you die, you will not be able to work or become productive). The ultimate result of the work of a Spirit-led life is such fruitfulness that men can see our light. Our work will vary with our talents: drafting policies, writing music, developing business ideas, making medical breakthroughs, showing personal ethics in the fields of law and politics, performing as a world-class athlete, designing buildings, teaching with a high pass rate, designing clothing, recognizing economic opportunities, balancing budgets, producing literature, and still more.

Then, like André Crouch, whose fruitful work through music influenced not only his generation but younger generations too, we can say, "To God be the glory for the things He has done."

Chapter 4

The Fruit-bearing Principle

ccording to the *Merriam-Webster Dictionary and Thesaurus*, the word principle has several definitions. Some of them include:

- A general of fundamental law, doctrine, or assumption
- A rule or code of conduct
- The laws or facts of nature underlying the working of an artificial device
- A primary source

In these definitions is a common thread: *original, foundation, first, source, beginning.* The prefix *princi-* means *first.* Therefore principles are basically essential and immutable original laws used as foundations for other philosophies.

The Word of God is a collection of books that contain principles. Everything in creation works by principles, and those principles are recorded in the Word of God for our benefit and admonition. One of those recorded principles is that of bearing fruit.

Bearing Fruit

The Biblical principle of bearing fruit is evident in Scripture. From the beginning of creation in Genesis, God set this fruit-bearing principle in motion, and it has not ceased. As it is written in Genesis 1:29: "And God said, Behold I have given you every herb bearing seed, which is upon the face of all the earth, and every tree, in the which is the fruit of a tree yielding seed; to you it shall be for meat."

We see here that the mighty Creator established the principle that fruit must be borne by any and every tree on the face of the earth. Why? Fruit indicates that the tree is alive and growing. The fruit is evidence that the tree has matured. The fruit contains seeds of that tree so that more of those trees can be planted. Then there will be no shortage of fruit-bearing trees on the earth!

So the purpose of bearing fruit is twofold: to indicate maturity and to reproduce more trees that bear fruit because fruitfulness glorifies God!

Of course, this is a natural example of how fruit-bearing trees work. Paul also commented on nature's manifestations of God's design.

> For ever since the creation of the world His invisible nature and attributes, that is, His eternal power and divinity, have been made intelligible and clearly discernible in and through the things that have been made (His handiworks). So [men] are without excuse [altogether without any defense or justification].
> —Romans 1:20 (AB)

In both Romans 15:4 and 1 Corinthians 10:6, Paul stated that everything in the Law (from Genesis through Deuteronomy) was written for our learning and spiritual application. This means that we can learn about the fruit-bearing principle and understand the nature of it by taking a look at the natural example of fruit bearing and then applying it spiritually. So let us examine how we can apply this principle spiritually.

"I see men as trees walking"

In Mark's gospel account is an interesting event worth mentioning here. The account is recorded as follows in Mark 8:22–26.

> And he cometh to Bethsaida; and they bring a blind man unto him, and besought him to touch him. And he took the blind man by the hand, and led him out of the town; and when he had spit on his eyes, and put his hands upon him, he asked him if he saw ought. And he looked up, and said, I see men as trees, walking. After that he put his hands again upon his eyes, and made him look up: and he was restored, and saw every man clearly. And he sent him away to his house, saying, Neither go into the town, nor tell it to any in the town.

Some people believe that Jesus made a mistake because He had to touch this blind man twice before he could see. However, I believe Jesus allowed this man to have a spiritual vision before restoring his natural vision. You see, fruit grows on trees. Spiritually, believers are referred to as trees. If believers are referred to as trees, then the implication here is that believers ought to bear fruit according to the fruit-bearing principle.

Read what the Word of God has to say about believers. Psalm 1:3 describes the characteristics of the blessed man: "And he shall be like a tree planted by the rivers of water, that bringeth forth his fruit in his season; his leaf also shall not wither; and whatsoever he doeth shall prosper."

In Psalm 92:12–14, the psalmist writes that the righteous "shall flourish like the palm tree: he shall grow like a cedar in Lebanon. Those that be planted in the house of the Lord shall flourish in the courts of our God. They shall still bring forth fruit in old age; they shall be fat and flourishing."

Isaiah also describes the recipients of God's salvation.

> The Spirit of the Lord God is upon me; because the Lord hath anointed me to preach good tidings unto the meek; he hath sent me to bind up the brokenhearted, to proclaim liberty to the captives, and the opening of the prison to them that are bound; To proclaim the acceptable year of the Lord, and the day of vengeance of our God; to comfort all that mourn; To appoint unto them that mourn in Zion, to give unto them beauty for ashes, the oil of joy for mourning, the garment of praise for the spirit of heaviness; that they might be called trees of righteousness, the planting of the Lord, that he might be glorified.
>
> —Isaiah 61:1–3

I believe that the Holy Spirit inspired Mark to record this particular event for our learning. You see, Jesus knew of the passages of Scripture mentioned earlier. In fact, when He had just begun His ministry, He read the one in Isaiah moments before He was expelled from the synagogue in Nazareth! Therefore, I believe that Jesus allowed this blind man to see, through the spirit, "men as trees walking" before giving him back his natural vision to illustrate a very important aspect of the fruit-bearing principle: ***There must be trees before there can be fruit.*** You cannot expect to have a harvest of mangoes or apples if there are no mango or apple trees. Likewise, you cannot expect to harvest spiritual fruit if there are no spiritual trees planted. It is quite evident from the previously mentioned passages that we, as believers, are spiritual trees of righteousness, planted by the chief Gardener. We are expected to bear fruit because fruit is an indication of maturity and the ability to produce more trees. Also, if we are spiritual trees of righteousness, the fruit we produce is the fruit of the Spirit (Galatians 5:22–23), the fruit of righteousness (James 3:18) and the "fruit" of good works (Matthew 5:16, Ephesians 2:10, 1 Peter 2:12).

Fruit is produced when growth is occurring.

When I was a child of about seven or eight years in Saint Martin, where I still live, my grandmother, who is a plant enthusiast, lived with us. One day while I was outside playing, she was tending to a new piece of bush that she had planted a few weeks earlier. Being the inquisitive young man that I was (and still am); I asked her what kind of plant it was.

"That is a peas tree," she said.

"A peas tree?" I responded. "Well, why doesn't it have any peas on it?"

She paused for a moment and then asked me, "Can you make children?"

"No," I said.

"Why not?"

"Because I'm not a grown-up yet."

"Exactly," she said. "Just as you can't make any children, because you are not a grown-up yet, the peas tree cannot make any peas, because it hasn't grown up yet."

Being the bright child I was, I said, "Oh, okay," and continued with whatever I had been doing.

Looking back at that conversation, her answer was so simple, yet so deep, that I didn't grasp it until years later when I became an adult. The Holy Spirit brought that memory back while I was studying these principles of growth for myself. That scene illustrated a simple, powerful reality and another aspect of the fruit-bearing principle to me. Yes, everything is designed to bear fruit; however, ***growth and maturity must be occurring before fruit can be produced.*** Fruit cannot be produced in a stage of non-growth. That is virtually impossible.

Enjoying the fruit

Please consider some verses on our topic.

> And this shall be a sign unto thee, Ye shall eat this year such as growth of itself; and the second year that which springeth of the same: and in the third year sow ye, and reap, and plant vineyards and eat the fruit thereof.
>
> —Isaiah 37:30

> And they shall build houses, and inhabit them; and they shall plant vineyards, and eat the fruit of them.
>
> —Isaiah 65:21

> He watereth the hills from his chambers: the earth is satisfied with the fruit of thy works.
>
> —Psalm 104:13

In these verses is yet another aspect of the fruit-bearing principle to note: ***fruit is meant to be eaten and enjoyed.*** The fruit is not eaten or enjoyed by the tree because it was not meant for the tree; the fruit is for the partakers of the tree. Take a look at Psalm 104:13 again. It says that the whole earth is satisfied with (enjoys) the fruit of God's labor. I do not know about you, but I eat and enjoy the fruit of God's labor every day, especially with my wife! If the fruit produced by you as a tree cannot be eaten or enjoyed by others, then it is not good fruit.

Different fruits for different groups

God illustrated this point during creation. In Genesis 2:9 we read that God created all the different kinds of trees, and all of them were not only good to look at, but good for food as well. Then, in

Genesis 2:16, we observe God telling Adam that he may eat of any and every tree in the garden except the tree of the knowledge of good and evil. Adam had choices. He did not have to eat the same fruit day after day. If he felt like eating mangoes today, that would not necessarily mean that he would want to eat mangoes tomorrow. He probably would have wanted to eat something else, like a banana or a grapefruit. Also, quite possibly, Adam may have taken a liking to certain trees because he enjoyed their fruit more than he did others. However, even if that were that case, that tree was still created as a good tree to bear good fruit.

In some instances, there will be groups of people who do not eat or enjoy the fruit produced by your tree. However, just because some people do not enjoy your fruit does not mean that it is not good fruit because ***not everybody likes the same fruit.*** That is another aspect we can derive from the fruit-bearing principle. I love mangoes, but I am not a big fan of oranges. Now the orange tree does not cry and get depressed because I do not like oranges, nor does it try to figure out why I don't like oranges and adapt itself so that I will like them. The orange tree continues to push out oranges at its appointed time, whether I like them or not. Likewise, the fruit you produce is not going to be liked and enjoyed by everybody. Many people will not like the fruit that comes from your tree, and your concern should never be those who do not particularly enjoy your type of fruit. Your concern should be to keep producing fruit so that those who do love to eat and enjoy your fruit are continuously satisfied. Remember, when you produce fruit, you are bringing glory to God because you are doing what He created you to do.

Violation of the fruit-bearing principle

When a mature tree bears no fruit, that is a violation of the fruit-bearing principle that God established. This is an abnormal occurrence because fruitless trees do not bring God the Creator the glory they should bring. God is the God of purpose, and He created everything with a purpose. God's glory is always revealed through purpose. If that purpose is not being fulfilled, God is not being glorified and He takes that very seriously.

Whenever principles are violated, there must be consequences. That is the natural order that God established. That is why Jesus said that if a branch does not bear fruit (fulfill its purpose), it will be cut off and discarded, as in John 15:2. Fruitlessness discredits God. If creation is supposed to declare the glory of God, how can a tree do that if it doesn't do what God created it to do? Every time you partake of the fruit of a tree, you are acting as a witness to the glory of God the Creator. A fruitless tree is a bad testimony before God, and He has no choice but to get rid of it.

That is also why Jesus cursed the fig tree in Matthew 21:18–20 and Mark 11:12–14.The cursing of the fig tree is pretty significant to me. Matthew wrote that when Jesus was on His way back to Jerusalem, He was hungry. On the journey He passed a fig tree. Hoping for figs, He found nothing but leaves. Mark adds a little more detail by informing the readers that "it was not the season for figs." When I read this, I became confused and I asked the Teacher why would Jesus curse the fig tree if it wasn't the season for figs? The Holy Spirit led me into research that proved to be extremely beneficial in my understanding of this passage.

In those days, these fig trees did not bear fruit during the Passover, which would be the modern day months of March or April. The season for figs was during the months of May and June, and that is when they bore fruit. However, fig trees generally produce a number of edible fruit buds in March, leaves in April, and ripe fruit during the months of May, June, and later on. So although the **season** for figs was not yet in progress, the **signs** of a fruitful season should have been evident. That would have indicated that the fruit-bearing principle was in operation.

Jesus, who was about to die very soon, probably desired to eat fruit from the fig tree one more time before He died, but He could not. He was not looking for the ripe fruit but for the edible buds. This tree was full of leaves but had no fruit buds. In Habakkuk 3:17 (NIV), the prophet writes, "Though the fig tree does not bud," and the rest of the passage goes on about fruitfulness, meaning that buds indicated a fruitful season ahead. The fact that there were no edible buds indicated that the tree would be fruitless that year. So Jesus cursed the fig tree for violating the fruit-bearing principle. One cannot know why it was barren; whatever the reasons were is between the tree and its Creator. However, its fruitlessness was a sign of something wrong according to the fruit-bearing principle. The tree's barrenness had the potential to discredit the Creator, so Jesus had to deal with it drastically.

So with the groundwork behind the fruit bearing principle laid, let us now take a look at the principles that can be derived from this original principle.

Chapter 5

Principles of Growth

In the previous chapter, we discovered that the Word of God is a collection of books that contain principles. Everything in creation works by principles, and those principles are recorded in the Word of God for our benefit and admonition. We also laid the foundation for understanding this fundamental principle of fruit bearing. Now let us discover the additional principles that support it.

Principle #1
We must desire to grow.

When a seed is planted in the ground, because of its design, it has to grow. In fact, its will to grow is so strong and fierce that it overcomes the initial obstacles of soil and gravity to break the surface. Then it still has to overcome the elements to continue growing. Why? The reason is simply because that seed has a desire to grow. We will never grow unless we first become like that seed and *desire* to grow. Here are some definitions of *desire* from the *Merriam-Webster Dictionary and Thesaurus:*

- To long or hope for
- A request
- A strong wish (longing)

Do you remember how badly you wanted to grow up when you were a child? I do. Children greatly desire to grow. That is indicated when they say things like, "I can't wait to grow up to be just like Daddy/Mommy/Stephen Curry," or "I can't wait till I'm eighteen so I can get my driver's license."

The prospect of being a mature adult fascinates children. They are dissatisfied with their current state because they know there is more to be achieved. The same principle applies in our spiritual lives. Unless we develop a holy dissatisfaction with where we are spiritually, we will not desire to grow and achieve more in and for the kingdom of God. Parents become so excited when their children learn something new—the first step, word, or drawing. Everyone wants children to develop new abilities because that is a positive sign that growth is taking place. Likewise, in spiritual matters, believers must *want* to grow. God's goal for you is to mature and develop the characteristics of Jesus Christ. First Peter 2:2 urges believers to grow—"As newborn babes, desire the sincere milk of the word, that ye may grow thereby."

Sadly, a common consensus is that many believers grow older in the faith but never grow up in the faith. They are stuck in a continuous spiritual infancy. They measure their spiritual progress by the number of years they have been "saved" rather than by the fruit that they should be producing. They never intended to grow. Some seem to like being spiritual babies. It's easy to be a baby with no responsibility; others feed you, clothe you, and change your diaper. But being a baby is not the goal of life. We are born babies so we can grow up and be productive and useful. Likewise, we are born again so we can become mature Christians, actively serving the Lord.

Maintenance is necessary

A second part to this first principle is this: We must maintain the desire to grow. Some believers who began the growth process may lose that desire. They make a hot start, on fire for the Lord, and get involved in every ministry. Then, over time, they lose their zeal. This could be due to several factors: lack of support or encouragement from other believers, not seeing changes happening in their lives, or other causes. Whatever the reasons may be, these are the believers who always appear at prayer meetings and in prayer lines, asking the pastor to pray for God to give them back the zeal they had in the beginning. This is an unscriptural prayer because nowhere does the Word say that God gives zeal. Zeal is something that every believer has to develop and nurture. As with faith, God only responds to the zeal that you portray. Zeal is defined in the *Merriam-Webster Dictionary and Thesaurus* as "eager and ardent interest in the pursuit of something (fervor)".

In some Scriptures, we see God responding to zeal: Hebrews 11:6, where God rewards the people who diligently seek Him; Psalm 119:2, where God blesses the people who seek Him with their whole heart; Revelation 3:19, where Jesus told the church at Laodicea that they needed to regain the zeal they lost, and when they did so, He would allow them to sit in positions of authority; and Jeremiah 33:3, where God said that He would answer those who called unto Him and show them great things that they did not know.

When people develop a burning desire to work for the Lord, they will then want to take the other steps needed for growth. Do you have that burning desire to accomplish more for the Lord? Have you set specific goals to accomplish for God, improvements to make, new levels to reach? If so, continue to nurture that zeal, because that is the indication that you desire, and maintaining that desire will enable the believer to grow and develop to maturity.

Principle #2
Growth is by choice.

If you are a believer, it is important that you know that God desires you to grow and mature. As a matter of fact, God wants us to grow into maturity. God does not want any spiritually immature children; He wants spiritually mature adults with whom He can communicate on an adult level. However, while God may want us to grow, He does not force us to grow. We have to make that choice on our own. Out of all of God's creation, the human species is the only one created with the ability to choose. Several scriptures indicate that we have the ability to choose. Two of these follow.

> I call heaven and earth to witness this day against you that I have set before you life and death, the blessings and the curses; therefore choose life that you and your descendants may live.
> —Deuteronomy 30:19 (AB)

> Death and life are in the power of the tongue: and they that love it shall eat the fruit thereof.
> —Proverbs 18:21 (KJV)

These verses show that we can choose whether or not to experience life and death or the blessings or the curses (judgment) of God. In

Proverbs 18:21, the phrase "eat the fruit thereof" implies that you choose whether or not to eat the fruit of life or the fruit of death. In the same respect, as believers, we also have a choice about growing spiritually.

I must note here that desiring growth is not the same as choosing to grow. Just because you have a desire to do something does not mean that you will choose to do it. For example, as a married man, I can certainly have the desire to have sex with my wife but choose not to because I'm busy working, studying, fasting, or doing some other activity that prevents me from being able to enjoy my wife at that moment. So it is with spiritual growth. You may actually have a genuine desire to grow spiritually, but if you do not make that conscious choice that says, "Hey, I have had enough," and start disciplining yourself and making choices that encourage growth, your desire to grow will remain just that, a desire. We grow old because aging is a mandatory fact of life but we grow up because we deliberately choose to do so.

Principle # 3
We must establish firm foundations for growth.

Psalm 82:5 states, "They know not, neither will they understand; they walk on in darkness: all the foundations of the earth are out of course."

Psalm 11:3 asks, "If the foundations be destroyed, what can the righteous do?"

Both verses refer to foundations. A foundation is a substructure upon which a building's structure is erected. You cannot "grow" or erect a building if no foundation is first laid. Why? The foundation supports the "growth" of the building. In fact, the entire "growing" process of the building depends on the foundation. If the foundation is sound and deep, the building will stand, no matter what comes against it. If not, when trouble occurs, the building will fall. Just as with physical structures, the same concept applies with spiritual structures. Spiritual structures can only be built strongly and soundly and be able to resist trouble if the foundations are properly laid.

Psalm 82:5 describes with perfect accuracy the world we live in today. "They know not, neither will they understand; they walk on in darkness." *Darkness*, in this context, indicates ignorance. Since the fall of Adam, the whole world has been in a state of ignorance. The gaps in our knowledge and comprehension have left us in a continuous state of ignorance.

As a result of that ignorance, "all the foundations of the earth are out of course." These foundations include individual, family, church, and national foundations. Psalm 11:3 poses a very pressing and crucial question that we tend to overlook sometimes: If all these foundations (individual, family, church, and national) that hold human society together are constantly undermined and destroyed, what hope is there for the righteous people? In other words, how much more difficult will life become for believers as a result of these destroyed foundations? I believe that is worth considering.

The solid rock

First Corinthians 3:11 also emphasizes a foundation: "For other foundation can no man lay than that is laid, which is Jesus Christ."

49

Before we can discuss building, we must first identify the best type of foundation for building. To date, the best foundation for a building is bedrock. Other less stable layers such as gravel, sand, soil, clay, and porous rock should be cut away so that a large structure can be built on bedrock. In our Christian lives, it is the same. Take a look at what 1 Corinthians 10:4 declares: "And did all drink the same spiritual drink: for they drank of that spiritual Rock that followed them: and that Rock was Christ."

Under the inspiration of the Spirit of God about Jesus, Isaiah 28:16 predicts, "Therefore thus saith the Lord God, Behold, I lay in Zion for a foundation a stone, a tried stone, a precious corner stone, a sure foundation: he that believeth shall not make haste."

We should not build anything unless we found it on Jesus Christ. He is the bedrock, and we should do and build nothing that He does not support. If we try to build something away from this truth, then the judgment day will bring it to light, because all that we have built will be tested. We will only receive a reward for what survives (1 Corinthians 3:10–15). Jesus will support only what He sees the Father doing (John 5:19). Therefore we must ask God the Father for His will for our lives and do only His will. Then we will have the assurance that Jesus will support our endeavor, and we can begin to build.

Rock or earth?

In Luke 6:46–49 we find an interesting parable Jesus used to illustrate the importance of foundations.

And why do you call me, Lord, Lord and do not the things which I say?

Whosoever cometh to me and heareth my sayings and doeth them, I will show you to whom he is like:

He is like a man which built a house, and digged deep, and laid the foundation on a rock: and when the flood arose, the stream beat vehemently upon that house, and it could not shake it: for it was founded upon a rock.

But he that heareth, and doeth not, is like a man that without a foundation built a house upon the earth; against which the stream did beat vehemently, and immediately it fell; and the ruin of that house was great.

This passage demonstrates clearly that we have a choice—remember Principle #2. We have the option of building our lives on rock or earth—stability or instability. It is important to lay good foundations because if they are not properly laid in the beginning, we run the risk of being like the foolish man who built his house on the sand. In this passage, rock represents truth and sand represents opinions.

Truth stands, no matter what comes against it, but opinions fail and falter with time. Jesus is saying that if you want to build on a good foundation, build on His words because His words are true (John 17:17) and do not build on the opinions and theories of others. So many people, including many Christians, are building their lives on unstable foundations such as materialism, ambitions, sports, education, political ideologies and philosophies, traditions of men, and human wisdom. The only stable, tried, and sure bedrock foundation is the Lord Jesus Christ, who is the Living Word and embodiment of truth. After all, Jesus did say that He is the Way, the Truth, and the Life in John 14:6.

Perfecting the saints

Why is it important to lay a good foundation? Ephesians 4:12–13 gives us the answer.

> For the perfecting of the saints, for the work of the ministry, for the edifying of the body of Christ:
>
> Till we all come in the unity of the faith, and of the knowledge of the Son of God, unto a perfect man, unto the measure of the stature of the fullness of Christ:

The foundations of our lives as Christians are so important that it is impossible to mature without them. Jesus wants us to be perfect (mature), just as He and His Father are perfect (mature) as emphasized in Matthew 5:48. If we will not lay the right foundations, we cannot expect to grow or develop to be as strong and mature as God would like us to be. God will not give us a "building permit" to continue the construction of our spiritual house if our foundations are inadequate. The reason is because when our structure falls, the ruin will be so great that it may claim other lives as well, and God will not allow any of His children to suffer at the hands of undeveloped believers.

So many believers are immature, even many who have been "saved" for years, because their foundations were never properly laid from the beginning. This is a tragedy because many of these people should now be teaching others or training their own disciples, but instead they are still spiritual babies in Christ, still needing spiritual milk instead of solid food, as mentioned in Hebrews 5:11–14.

God wants us to lay the right foundations so that we can grow in maturity in Him so that we can then go out to teach and edify disciples, others in the body of Christ.

Principle #4
We must embrace change to experience growth.

If we want to grow up spiritually, there are lifestyle changes that we must make to create an environment conducive to growth. However, many people fear change. Change often leaves a bad taste in people's mouths when it is mentioned. However, experiencing growth means that we must be open and adaptable enough to embrace change because change is the introduction of the future to the present. When those introductions begin, if we are not prepared to embrace change, we will get left behind and wonder what happened.

I have found that many people view change negatively because most are not taught how to manage, embrace, and maximize change. People are not born knowing how to manage and handle change. Change also pulls people out of their comfort zones. Humans are creatures of habit. When something or someone threatens to draw us away from what we consider normal, we may become defensive and say, "This is who I am, and I'm not going to change."

Ironically, some of us say that we want to grow, but that is impossible without change. If we want to grow, we cannot view change as negative. The Word of God lets us know, in Malachi 3:6 and Genesis 8:22, that two constants are God and change. In Malachi 3:6, God says, "For I am the Lord, I change not." Genesis 8:22 mentions natural, cyclical change: "While the earth remaineth, seedtime and harvest, and cold and heat, and summer and winter, and day and night shall not cease."

Last time I checked, the earth is still here and so it is safe to assume that nature's changes still occur on schedule. This also means that everything associated with the earth undergoes change as well. Human life is one big cycle of change from baby to adult, daycare to a job, single life to marriage, and novice to expert in any profession. Change is built into everything that we do. This is because God is pro-change. If He was not, then He would not have designed everything with the ability to change.

I must mention here that when we say God does not change, we refer to His character and His attributes—the characteristics that define Him as God. His faithfulness, trustworthiness, righteousness, and loving kindness are the constants we mean when we say, "God is the same yesterday, today, and forever." His character and attributes do not change. However, when it comes to His purpose and accomplishing His purpose in every generation, His methods change. God is to creative and dynamic to use the same technique twice. Therefore change is essential to us, as growing believers, in order to bear fruit and fulfill God's purpose in each generation.

Before a seed becomes the tree it was made to be, it has to undergo massive changes. Therefore, before we can become all that God designed us to be, we must be willing to change behaviors and attitudes that can hinder us from maturing as believers.

Benefits of embracing change

The moment we alter our negative outlook on change, we will begin to realize the awesome benefits of embracing and anticipating change. These points are just a few benefits that come as a result of embracing change. I discovered them by examining the life of David, the second king of Israel.

1. Embracing change exposes the need for personal growth.

Embracing change exposes the need for growth in a particular area of your life. For David, it was in the area of his faith. He constantly experienced God's hand of protection on his life. For several years, David was pursued relentlessly by Saul, whose sole aim was to kill him. It was during these difficult times that David found solace and strength in God by writing poems and songs to encourage himself in the Lord. His psalm writing helped his faith in God grow as he experienced God's deliverance from Saul time and time again. Had David not experienced this side of Saul, he would have never known his need to grow in faith and trust in the Lord God of Israel. Now we have almost seventy-five percent of the largest book of praise and worship in the Bible attributed to David as a result of his growth in faith.

2. Embracing change presents opportunities.

Opportunities you never knew existed come as a result of embracing change. David never expected to get an audience with the king.

However, because he was willing to stop tending sheep, he became King Saul's personal musician. After that audience, more opportunities became available to David because he was willing to change.

3. Embracing change uncovers potential.

You don't know what you are made of until change occurs. The passage found in 1 Samuel 16:14–19 is very fascinating. It reveals the truth of this point very clearly.

> But the Spirit of the Lord departed from Saul, and an evil spirit from the Lord troubled him. And Saul's servants said unto him, Behold now, an evil spirit from God troubleth thee. Let our lord now command thy servants, which are before thee, to seek out a man, who is a cunning player on an harp: and it shall come to pass, when the evil spirit from God is upon thee, that he shall play with his hand, and thou shalt be well. And Saul said unto his servants, Provide me now a man that can play well, and bring him to me. Then answered one of the servants, and said, Behold, I have seen a son of Jesse the Bethlehemite, that is cunning in playing, and a mighty valiant man, and a man of war, and prudent in matters, and a comely person, and the Lord is with him. Wherefore Saul sent messengers unto Jesse, and said, Send me David thy son, which is with the sheep.

I believe God set that moment up just so that David could be discovered and identified and also so that the entire nation of Israel saw what

David, the next anointed king, was made of. The passage shows us the potential that David had because when the evil spirit began to torment Saul—when the king's emotional situation changed—he needed a skillful musician to calm him.

His son Solomon probably heard this story a thousand times, which probably inspired him to write in Proverbs 18:16 that "a man's gift maketh room for him, and bringeth him before great men." Until David was discovered, he sat in the sheep pen tending sheep, but when Saul's servants saw the gifts and potential of the young man, his abilities brought him before the king.

4. Embracing change brings progress.

If something is progressing, that means it is moving. If it is moving, it is changing. So change indicates progress. If there is no change, then there is no progress. The path to David's kingship was not easy. It featured one test, trial, and tribulation after the other, but that did not deter David from advancing. David made consistent progress. Through many hard times, struggles, and setbacks, he persevered until he ultimately became king.

It is clear from the Scriptures that spiritual growth is not automatic. It takes an intentional commitment. You must desire to grow; you must choose to grow and make an effort to grow by building on firm foundations. Furthermore, you must embrace changes in your life to create and maximize the environments necessary for growth. You must also be able to recognize some conditions that do not promote the growth you seek. We will examine these hindrances in the next chapter.

Chapter 6

Hindrances of Growth

Many times, both knowingly and unknowingly, as believers we sabotage our own growth and ability to bear fruit. I have seen many believers of all ages cheat themselves out of growth and maturation in the faith and the fruitful results of maturation. This is very sad. Many of these people end up in vicious cycles of defeat—marvelous potential and possibility unharnessed, lives and purposes unfulfilled. The sad reality of this is if they have children, they pass their thought processes to the next generation, not necessarily by their words but by their actions.

Their words say, "Go to school and get a good education so that you can be somebody." Meanwhile, though, their actions encourage playing the lottery, drinking, partying, and living a frivolous life because of this absolutely ridiculous YOLO (You Only Live Once) philosophy, which is perpetuated by pop-culture celebrities of this present generation. When the parental words and the parental behavior contradict each other, the child is naturally confused. That is why we must learn to identify the hindrances to growth so that we can eliminate them. This is how we will preserve the next generation. Otherwise, they will suffer as a result of our inability to grow and mature.

A major reason Christians do not grow is that they do not see the need for growth. That is a big roadblock to development. They have no desire to work and serve to the full extent of their ability. They develop a spirit of indifference or negligence. Another reason is that, after they develop a certain level of maturity, they stagnate. They become satisfied, thinking no more growth is needed. This belief is satanic in origin because God created everything to grow and develop. The Scriptures teach us that growth is essential, so the notion that one has arrived is biblically false and satanic.

The following list is not all-inclusive. However, if you find yourself suffering from any of the following influences, you may be sabotaging your own growth. This list is meant to help believers identify the areas in their lives that need more work. So if you feel a sense of condemnation come over you, realize that such condemnation is not the work of the Holy Spirit and shake that feeling off in the name of Jesus!

Hindrances to growth

Tradition

One of the major hindrances to growth is traditionalism. "This is how we have always done it" expresses this viewpoint. I have come to define tradition as "a previously successful move of God that has been turned into a ritual." If we are not vigilant, our traditions can nullify the effectiveness of the Word of God in our lives. Mark 7:13 explains this clearly: "Making the word of God of none effect through your tradition, which ye have delivered: and many such like things do ye."

The Word of God is seed, as in Luke 8:11. Whenever seed is planted, it is expected to grow. When we allow traditionalism to take the place that the Word of God is supposed to have, we can get so stuck in tradition that it actually hinders the movement of the Spirit in our lives. It is the movement of the Spirit that enables us to grow. Tradition chokes the seed and prevents it from growing and producing what it was designed to produce in our lives.

This is also evident in churches so attached to traditional practices that they are left behind. They took what God gave them as a revelation for yesterday and turned it into a tradition that nullifies the Word of God today. As a result, there is no life in their assemblies; there are no demonstrations of power. People leave these assemblies the same way they came—or sometimes even worse because of traditionalism in the church.

Negative Thinking

We can unknowingly choke our own growth with negative thoughts. All of us are a sum total of the thoughts that we think. Therefore it is no small wonder that the apostle Paul advised us, in Romans 12:2, to "be not be conformed to this world: but be ye transformed by the renewing of your mind that you may prove what is that good and acceptable and perfect will of God."

Paul is strongly advising that believers change the way they think. Why? If we don't change the way we think, we cannot prove (manifest) what the will of God is. In order to understand God, His Word, His purpose, and His concepts, it requires a change in our thinking process. Some concepts in the Word will be difficult to understand unless we change the way we think about them.

Negative thoughts can become negative words, and we all know our words have power. Negative thinking can keep us bound in cycles of hopelessness and despair. We think that if we expect the worst, then we will not be as disappointed if events do not turn out as we had hoped. But when the outcomes are worse than expected, we still get depressed because we didn't expect the playout to be that bad either! What a bewildering state! It is time that believers stop speaking in a way that is inconsistent with what we want. Life is far better when we keep a positive mindset because a positive mindset says, "No matter what comes, it cannot be like this forever."

Mediocrity

Many believers have settled for this false idea that being great is ungodly and so remain in a state of mediocrity for the rest of their lives. This is nothing short of an insult to God because He is not a mediocre being, nor did He create anything to be mediocre either! People have this false view of greatness because of bad teaching in the church.

In the book of Matthew, we read about the day that Jesus and the disciples were out doing ministry and a discussion arose, concerning who was the greatest and who would be the greatest. When they asked Jesus what His thoughts on the matter were, He threw them a curve ball they didn't expect.

> But Jesus called them unto him and said, Ye know that the princes of the Gentiles exercise dominion over them, and they that are great exercise authority upon them. But it shall not be so among you: but whosoever will be great among you let him be your minister; And whosoever will be chief among you, let him be your servant: Even as the Son of man came not to be ministered unto, but to minister, and to give his life a ransom for many.
>
> —Matthew 20:25–26

A closer look at the passage reveals that Jesus never rebuked the disciples' desire for greatness. He simply redirected it. He basically said that greatness is to be desired, but not for the wrong reasons. God wants us to be great, but not to the point where we might take the glory that is designed for God for ourselves. That is a vital point. That is where greatness crosses the boundary over into pride territory, an area that God detests very much. We were never designed for mediocrity, and God expects greatness from us because He is great and He created us in His image. Being great is putting God's work in your life on display so others can see His handiwork and give Him glory for the fruit your life produces. Mediocrity stops growth. Balked growth hinders your greatness, which ultimately blocks God from displaying His greatness through you.

Complacency

When complacent, a person or an organization begins to die a very slow death. A complacent culture is toxic because it has to do with self-satisfaction—contentment with the current state of things. If you are content with current conditions that means you see no immediate need to change or continue moving toward the ideal. The complacent are quick to make excuses about current conditions. If you rely on experience rather than respond to new information, or if you cannot take correction from others, you have become complacent. Complacency is deadly because most people and organizations that are complacent don't realize when it has set in. Sometimes they do not realize that they have become complacent until someone informs them. All of us, in some way, are complacent. We just need to be made aware of that complacency so that we can begin to deal with it effectively.

Carnal behavior

Often we encounter situations that make us ask if some professing Christians really are who they say they are! Though the point is seldom addressed, there are really two kinds of Christians in the world: carnally-minded Christians and spiritually-minded Christians.

In Romans 8:6, Paul defined the consequences of carnality: "For to be carnally minded is death; but to be spiritually minded is life and peace." Then he brings up the discussion again in first letter to the Corinthian church.

> And I, brethren, could not speak unto you as unto spiritual, but as unto carnal, even as unto babes in Christ. I have fed you with milk, and not with meat: for hitherto ye were not able to bear it, neither yet now are ye able. For ye are yet carnal: for whereas

there is among you envying, and strife, and divisions,

are ye not carnal, and walk as men?

—1 Corinthians 3:1–3

Paul asks in verse 3, "For ye are yet carnal: for whereas there is among you envying, and strife, and divisions, are ye not carnal, and walk as men?" That is the mark of carnality. Where there is extensive and excessive strife in any Christian-based organization, there are carnal Christians. Strife is the mark of carnality—they can't get along with other Christians. Carnal Christians try to achieve their goals by their own strength instead of relying on the power of the Spirit to help them.

Guilt and condemnation

These are by far the Devil's biggest and favorite tools. He loves to remind us of our mistakes. Guilt only reminds us of who we were yesterday, not who we can be tomorrow. Condemnation makes sure that we constantly beat ourselves up because of that memory. The Devil does not play fair when it comes to this.

As maturing believers, we will inevitably encounter the people I call "the rememberers." These people constantly remind you of who you were, where you were, how they helped you, and so on and so forth. This would not be so bad except that the rememberers remind you of your past for a purpose. They don't commend you on the progress you are making; they harp on the mistakes you still make. They use their memories to prove you are not ready for the future and that you will always need them. This can be dangerous because it can make you second-guess yourself and over think your decisions.

The rememberers can make a person condemn him or herself, and mistakes then overshadow progress and hinder growth.

As believers, we should neither condemn ourselves nor allow anyone else to do so because Romans 8:1 adjures us: "There is therefore now no condemnation to them which are in Christ Jesus, who walk not after the flesh, but after the Spirit."

This means that as born-again believers, if you believe by faith that the finished work of Jesus Christ was fulfilled on your behalf, you don't have the right to condemn yourself. Neither does anyone else. The day you became born again and the Holy Spirit took up residence inside you, you became a new creation, free from the guilt of wrongdoing and of condemnation for the wrongdoing. God also personally guarantees that He is committed to completing the work He started in you the day you were born again, as stated in both 2 Corinthians 5:17 and Philippians 1:6. If God Almighty, who has all rights to condemn people, does not do it, who are we to do it to ourselves and others? In John 3:17, Jesus Himself said that He did not come to the world to condemn it, but to save it.

We have direct Scriptural advice to protect ourselves from the rememberers.

> Brethren, I count not myself to have apprehended: but this one thing I do, forgetting those things which are behind, and reaching forth unto those things which are before, I press toward the mark for the prize of the high calling of God in Christ Jesus.
>
> —Philippians 3:13–14

In other words, don't let the fear of the past stop you from growing and moving on toward the high calling, which is perfection (maturity) as a believer. The worst thing you can do is allow the crippling effect of condemnation to stunt your growth. That is where some of us get caught in the web of lies the Devil spins for us. Remember, it is the Holy Spirit's job, through the Word of God, to fix everything that is wrong with you, not your job. So when the Holy Spirit deals with you in a particular area in your life, acknowledge it, deal with it, and move on from there. Don't dwell on it. That opens the door for condemnation, which leads to depression and a whole host of other issues. God forgives us, but we must learn to forgive ourselves. Shut the door in condemnation's face today!

Fear

The movie *After Earth*, starring Will Smith and his son Jaden, tells the story of a father and son, Cypher and Kitai, who crash-land on Earth a thousand years after calamitous events forced humanity to abandon the planet. After so many years, the earth has become a hostile territory, with more lethal plant and animal species and unpredictable weather changes. The crash leaves both Cypher's legs broken. The only way for both Cypher and Kitai to escape safely is for Kitai to find his way alone across the hostile terrain to retrieve a locator beacon to signal for help. Needless to say, with all the deadly evolutions, Kitai is frightened as he embarks on the expedition. Cypher gives his son advice about fear that I believe is both true and relevant to us as believers. He says, "You must realize that fear is not real. It (fear) is a product of the thoughts you create. Do not misunderstand me, danger is very real, but fear is a choice."

The apostle Paul echoed this very same sentiment more than two thousand years earlier when he told Timothy, in 2 Timothy 1:7, "For God hath not given us the spirit of fear; but of power, and of love, and of a sound mind."

Fear is a crippling emotion that prevents growth because it makes people reluctant to leave the environments and situations they know well. Fear programs the mind for failure and makes us expect the worst before we even try. Fear is a leading cause of choked growth, abandoned dreams, and unharnessed potential. Fear keeps us from growing because we become more conscious of what other people will think about us when they see us excelling and moving forward. So we resign ourselves to stunted growth because we don't want to stand out from the crowd.

We can choose whether or not to fear. If we fear, our fear becomes a roadblock that stops us from experiencing the life we were created to live. If we don't, we remove the chains the spirit of fear has placed on us and walk in power, love, and sound, clear thinking. This fear-free mindset will help us produce all the fruit linked to that growth; this includes the application of talents, realization of dreams, attainment of goals, operation of businesses, and all useful and creative human endeavors. Remember the old saying, "You never know if you'll succeed until you try!"

Before you decide not to do something because of fear, please do me a personal favor and think of how much growth potential and achievement will go to the grave with you because of fear.

Neglect

Many believers do not experience growth simply because of neglect. They haven't bothered to keep themselves spiritually fit. They have stopped praying, stopped coming to church, stopped coming to small group Bible study. They have completely neglected and starved their spiritual being and have begun drifting along the current of life with everyone else.

Proverbs 4:23 instructs us, "Keep thy heart with all diligence; for out of it are the issues of life."

In this verse, *heart* is synonymous with *spirit*, and *to keep* means *to protect*. So the verse tells us, "Protect your spirit with all diligence." We have to make a constant effort to protect our spiritual selves and keep building them, making a diligent effort to avoid neglect of any aspect of our spiritual lives. If believers want to see growth in their lives, neglect is a very deadly hindrance that must be overcome.

Disobedience

Sometimes believers don't see growth in their lives because God has asked them to do something and is patiently waiting until they decide to do it. That last instruction probably has a link to your growth.

First Samuel 15:22 has advice on obedience: "And Samuel said, Hath the Lord as great delight in burnt offerings and sacrifices, as in obeying the voice of the Lord? Behold, to obey is better than sacrifice, and to hearken than the fat of rams."

Here the Lord is saying, through the prophet Samuel, that He would rather people obey Him and His Word than worship Him because, in carrying out and fulfilling His Word, believers are actually worshipping Him. However, when you decide to just offer up "worship" and not obey God's Word, your "worship" becomes a stench to God, as He said several times to Old Testament prophets. It became a stench because the people were offering sacrifices but not obeying the Word, which has the power to bring about growth and transformation. So the worship was just a performance. It was not authentic because the condition of their hearts was not right. They were still disobedient to God's Word.

Compromise

These are the believers who have allowed the "little foxes that spoil the vine," mentioned in Song of Songs 2:15, to come in. "Foxes" might be compromised values, morals, and ethics. Believers make such compromises when in a snare designed by the enemy. The results of their compromises interfere with their walk with God and hinder their growth. They are trying to live a life balanced between pleasing themselves and pleasing God. Instead of having a fruitful, fulfilled life in service to God, filled with consistent growth, they end up frustrated and dissatisfied, pleasing neither themselves nor God.

If you find yourself experiencing one or more of the items on this list, take a moment to ask God to help you overcome these characteristics so that you can begin to experience the growth and, by extension, the fruitful life that God desires us to experience.

Prayer for overcoming hindrances

Heavenly Father, please help me to overcome these deadly characteristics that would cause me to miss out on the wonderful things you have for me. Your Word says that you will bless me exceedingly, abundantly, and above all that I can ask or think. Help me to remember that your promises are true and you always have and always will provide for my every need. Let this promise be a reminder to me when I feel that I am unworthy and undeserving. Most importantly, help me to keep the faith so that I will always please you. In Jesus' name, amen!

Part II

Keys to Experiencing Growth and Bearing Fruit

Introduction to Part II

Use Your Keys!

H ave you ever misplaced your keys? Do you remember how you felt after realizing that you misplaced them and could not unlock your house or start your car? I've observed people who have locked themselves out of their cars. Many of them get extremely upset, frustrated, embarrassed, and disgusted with themselves.

Keys represent three interlocking ideas—access, authority, and control. For example, if I were an audio/visual engineer for a company, I would need access to the audio and video equipment storage area. A key would give me that access. That key would then give me the ability to use that equipment along with the responsibility for that equipment. That authority carries control.

If more than one person has a key to a particular area, then the access, authority, and control is shared and equal among the key holders. Not all of them may use it equally well. For example, if a colleague and I both have keys to the audio/video equipment area, but my colleague has more advanced knowledge about the equipment than I do, he or she can use the equipment more effectively and efficiently than I can.

That is the reason why I believe many believers are frustrated and stagnating. The kingdom of God has all the equipment we will ever need for a life full of growth and productivity. We all have the keys and the same level of access, authority, and control when it comes to the kingdom. However, we may not know about the keys available to us, and therefore we cannot use them. Or we may know about the keys but do not use them as effectively and efficiently as others may. Either way, we may become depressed or give up.

As citizens, we have to be aware of the different keys provided to us by the kingdom for our growth and benefit. In this next section, I am going to provide some keys that I have used in my own life and ways to use the equipment to experience growth and maximum productivity. There are different keys to unlock the power of different sections of the kingdom and make the kingdom work in our lives. I believe that the following keys will unlock the power that brings transformational growth and productivity in believers' lives if believers will use them effectively and efficiently. When we begin to make use of the following kingdom keys, the kingdom will work in our lives as it is designed to do, and we will begin to experience growth and fruitfulness in all areas of our lives.

Chapter 7

Key #1:
Read the Word

At the time of this writing, I had recently received a computer from a good friend. It was a timely gift for two reasons: My laptop was almost nine years old at the time, and I needed a computer with more memory to handle the growth of our emerging ministry. There was a program that I needed on the computer to produce some work for the ministry, however I had to download the software package for this work. From that experience I got a revelation: Even though I had the necessary hardware, it was useless while it lacked the required software. It needed that software to perform the tasks I intended.

That is why I believe the first key to positioning yourself for spiritual growth and productivity is reading the Word. Reading the Word is the equivalent of downloading the software. You don't use the software all the time. However, when you do, you can retrieve information readily because it is saved. For example, you may not need to use the software of healing, deliverance, or prosperity often, but if you have downloaded it, it is there when you need to retrieve it. You are a spirit being, and the Word of God is a spirit word, as it is written in John 6:63. So when you read the Bible, you download the Word of God into your spirit because only spiritual beings can comprehend and discern spiritual matters, as it is written in 1 Corinthians 2:10–14. After this download, the Holy Spirit can now bring everything Jesus taught back to your memory when you need it because it is already stored in your memory, as explained in John 14:26.

People like to memorize Scripture verses and think that will help them in tough times. Memorizing verses is good, but Jesus said it is not your job to remember them; it is the Holy Spirit's job to do that. Our job is to "hide the Word in our heart," as mentioned in Psalm 119:11. If we replace *heart* with *spirit,* the verse will make more sense. We hide the Word in our hearts by constantly reading and meditating on it. In the next chapter, we are going to discuss the controversial topic of praying in tongues, but for now I'll just briefly mention it. Reading and meditation on the Word coupled with prayer in tongues is a very potent combination. When you pray in tongues, you are praying in faith for something you cannot yet identify. Since the Holy Spirit is within you, He can now look in your software, retrieve the information you need, and shed light on it—and you grow into a deeper relationship with God. What an awesome combination!

However, if we are going to use the Word of God to grow, we first have to know what the Word of God is, its purpose, and its impact on the lives of those who read it.

What is the Word of God?

The Word of God is the manifestation of the mind and the will of God. A word is a manifested thought. Jesus alluded to this fact in Matthew 12:34. He asked the religious leaders of the day, "O generation of vipers, how can ye, being evil, speak good things? for out of the abundance of the heart the mouth speaketh."

Words give insight on who a person really is because they reflect what that person thinks, both positive and negative thoughts. Thoughts are so powerful that the Word tells us, in Proverbs 23:7, "For as he <u>thinketh</u> in his heart, so is he."

We are all the total of the thoughts that we think. Therefore, the way we speak reflects what and how we think about ourselves. Everything we say or withhold, whether good or bad, is a result of what and how we think. Everything is subject to the interpretation of what we think. Therefore if what we think is incorrect, then our words, actions, and lifestyles will also be incorrect.

Through the prophet Isaiah, God revealed to us the connection between His thoughts and His Word.

> For my thoughts are not your thoughts, neither are your ways my ways, saith the Lord. For as the heavens are higher than the earth, so are my ways higher than your ways, and my thoughts than your thoughts. For as the rain cometh down, and the snow from heaven, and returneth not thither, but watereth the earth, and maketh it bring forth and bud, that it may give seed to the sower, and bread to the eater: So shall my word be that goeth forth out of my mouth: it shall not return unto me void, but it shall accomplish

that which I please, and it shall prosper in the thing whereto I sent it.

—Isaiah 55:8–11

In verse 8 God says that His thoughts are not like our thoughts because His are higher. These thoughts are in God's mind, and we do not know what is in the mind of God. Only the Spirit of God knows what's in the mind of God, as specified in 1 Corinthians 2:11. We can only understand these higher thoughts if they are translated into words. The Spirit of God does this, using mankind as a vessel, because spirits cannot utter physical words.

Here is a paraphrase of God's words in verse 11: "I think on a different level than you, so you don't know what is on my mind. However, I'm going to let you know what is on my mind. Using Isaiah as a mouthpiece, I am going to speak what is on my mind, and you will know that these are my thoughts because I speak what I am thinking, and whatever I speak will not come back without doing what it was spoken to do. That is how you will know what is on my mind, what is my will, my intention, and my purpose." So the Word of God, either written or spoken, is God's mind, will, intention, and purpose. His Word gives us insight into what God is like.

What is the purpose of the Word of God?

The Word helps us to grow and mature through encouragement, instruction, and correction, as is written in 2 Timothy 3:16–17. The Word is the proverbial measuring stick for growth. People, families, churches, and nations are in their current chaos because they have replaced the standard of the Word of God with their opinions. Judges 17:26 and 21:25 describe exactly what we are facing now: "Everyone did what was right in his own eyes." There was no standard from God operating in society. If people rely on their flawed logic, worldviews, vantage points, and opinions and leave the Word out, no true and authentic growth can occur in their lives. Before we can experience growth, we accept the Word as the final authority in our lives. It has to be the foundation for everything about us, or we will be attempting to grow on the unstable foundations of opinions, views, and emotions. This is precisely the reason why I listed reading the Word as the first essential key for growth.

As the absolute standard, the Word enables us to evaluate ourselves and determine where we are and what we need to do to move forward. What are we measuring ourselves and our growth against? Are we measuring it against what the world is saying, or are we measuring it against what the Word is saying?

What is the impact of reading the Word?

The impact of reading the Word is threefold. It renews minds, brings change, and advances the kingdom of God on earth.

Renewing the mind

Reading the Word gives people an opportunity to observe what God's standard is. Reading the Word is the only way to understand what and how God thinks. This is how we can begin to interpret kingdom concepts rightly. We must take Paul's advice in Romans 12:2—"And be not conformed to this world: but be ye transformed by the renewing of your mind, that ye may prove what is that good, and acceptable, and perfect, will of God."

Renewing the mind is not only talking about putting the Word in us, although that is of paramount importance; it means allowing the Word to change the way we think about and view certain things. If we are to understand God, His Word, and His purpose, then transformation is the order of the day. Transformation by the renewal of our minds is known as one word—repentance, which we will discuss further in the next chapter. This is the same message the prophets, John the Baptist, Jesus, and the apostles preached during their public ministries. To repent literally means to experience a change of heart (spirit); this inspires a change of mind that results in a change of direction. Our hearts (spirits) are changed instantly because of our decision to follow Jesus and submit to Him, as in 2 Corinthians 5:7. If, however, we don't take time to renew our minds, they will still remain the same. To begin renewing our minds, we have to allow the Word of God to be the final authority in our lives. In James 1:21, the apostle James writes that we are to receive the engrafted Word of God that is able to save our souls. The soul represents the mental and emotional capacities. In 1 Peter 2:2, the apostle Peter writes that we are to desire the sincere milk of the Word in order to grow. All this has to do with renewing our minds and changing the way we think.

The Word brings change

The Word and proper application of the Word will always bring about change in people's lives. Application of revealed knowledge of the truth of God's Word brings freedom and transformation, as stated in John 8:31–32. The reason most believers are defeated by life's problems is probably because of any or all of three factors.

1. They do not know the Word.
2. They do not know how to apply the Word.
3. They refuse to apply the Word that they know.

If any of these three factors apply to a believer, his chance for growth will be slim because he lacks what is necessary for change to occur in his life.

The Word advances the kingdom

Reading the Word exposes us to the kingdom lifestyle and allows believers to gain access into the kingdom by providing an alternative perspective. In Colossians 3:2 (AB), it is written: "And set your minds and keep them set on what is above (the higher things), not on the things that are on the earth." The same verse in the Message Bible advises us that we should "see things from His perspective."

The word *His* in this verse refers to the King of Kings: Jesus Christ, the one who has all authority in heaven and earth. This verse indicates that we should keep focused on seeing events from the vantage point of the King despite all the worldly distractions. So what does this mean? How can we view events from the perspective of the King and His kingdom?

Matthew 6:33 (AB) explains, "But seek (aim at and strive after) first of all His kingdom and His righteousness (His way of doing and being right), and then all these things taken together will be given you besides."

This verse unlocks the solution to many issues plaguing us today. This means that in whatever situations we confront, whether on a personal, family, church, or national level, we must attempt to understand the situation from the King's perspective (His kingdom) and His way of handling it (His righteousness). To do that, we must read the Word to learn what the King has to say about our dilemma.

These are definitions of seek taken from the *Merriam-Webster Dictionary and Thesaurus*.

1. to search for
2. to try and reach or obtain
3. to make an attempt

We must take time to seek earnestly in the Word of God for what the King has to say about the personal, family, church, or national situations we confront (His kingdom) and the way to apply the Word to our unique situations (His righteousness). Then we will obtain the results, improvements, and changes we want. Too often we want to put the cart before the horse and then expect God to work a miracle. Most of the time, our problem is that we don't want to take the time to seek the King's perspective on the issue—or, when we have identified the King's perspective, we don't want to apply His perspective to our situations.

Finding out what the King has to say is knowledge. Knowledge is good, but the application of knowledge is wisdom, and wisdom is even better. That is why Proverbs 4:7 stresses that wisdom is our most important goal, but that to get wisdom, we must get understanding. We must strive for wisdom even if it costs us everything we have because we cannot apply knowledge we do not understand. This whole thrust toward wisdom advances the kingdom of God.

God will not show Himself because He already has manifested through His Word. We must take the time to become familiar with His Word, study it, and realize the power and authority that we have in our hands every time we open the Bible. Revelation 1:6 and 5:10 characterize believers as kings and priests. If we, as kings and priests, begin to speak the same Word as the King of Kings, we can harness that same power and authority in our lives as well. The written Word of God is the most powerful document we have. We must learn it and behave according to it for it to benefit us.

Chapter 8

Key #2:
Develop a Prayer Life

I know the phrase above seems clichéd, but it is valid. It is number two because prayer now activates the first point of reading the Word. We must get a good understanding of what prayer is, but first let us discover what prayer is not. Prayer is not a religious act. Prayer is not only for old people. Prayer is not something you do only when you are in trouble and are in need of a quick way out. Finally, prayer is not something you do when you are about to take an exam but have not studied. Prayer goes much further than that. Prayer is the most essential part of any believer's life for one simple reason—it is how believers communicate with God. Prayer is a critical component of believers' lives and enables them to access all that is necessary for growth and fruitfulness.

The purpose of prayer is to help us become better individuals through the help of the Holy Spirit that lives in us. Prayer does more for us than it does for God. Prayer does not move God to do anything. Prayer changes us and places us in a position to be used by Him for His glory. Prayer involves God placing Himself at our disposal to help us grow and mature so that we can effectively fulfill our duty to His kingdom's purpose. It is important that we understand that we don't pray to earn God's favor or to bring His judgment; we pray to release it into the earth as it is written in Matthew 6:10: "Thy kingdom come. Thy will be done on earth, as it is in heaven." God's favor has already been granted. Likewise, His judgment has already been delivered. He just needs willing vessels, such as ourselves, to implement it on earth.

It is interesting to note that, among Jesus' activities and miracles witnessed by His disciples over three and a half years, prayer is the only one on record that they asked Jesus to teach them how to do. Jesus walked on water; healed deaf, dumb, and blind people; cast out demons; fed thousands of people at one time through miraculous means; and even raised people from the dead. Yet the disciples' only request was, "Lord, teach us how to pray." This simple fact alone is an indication of how important prayer is or should be to us. There are some principles of prayer that I find very helpful in the believer's quest for growth. These three areas are repentance, confession, and application.

Repentance

Repentance is a term that has been grossly misinterpreted and subsequently misunderstood and misused. The Greek word for *repentance* is the verb *metanoeo* (Strong 3340), which means *to change one's mind or purpose*. In elementary school grammar, we learn that a verb is a word that is associated with action. An important aspect of *metanoeo* is that its tense denotes an action that is continuous. So when the word *repent* is mentioned, it is not referring to the action of coming to the front of a church, weeping and wailing and letting everyone know about your private life. Repentance is an internal decision to change one's mindset or outlook on certain issues; repentance denotes an action that is always taking place. So repentance is an action within one's thoughts.

So, when we use the term accurately, *repent* means *to change your mind.* Changing one's mind, in itself, is incomplete repentance because a person can change his or her mind about an incorrect action and still do it. In the Bible, repentance means changing one's mind about sin in such a way as to result in a change of action. Repentance means taking our thoughts, setting them on the Word of God, and letting the Word change our thoughts if our thoughts don't line up with the Word. This is why reading the Word is as important as key #1: Everything begins with the Word of God, the foundation upon which all else is built. However, because we don't take the time to read and let the Word enter us, our minds don't change. Consequently, our directions do not change either. True repentance results in a change of direction. If we have not changed direction, how can we say that we have truly repented? Just because you have been born again does not mean that you have repented sufficiently. John and Jesus preached, "Repent, for the kingdom of God is at hand." That was Jesus' first recorded public message. This is essentially what Jesus said when He began His ministry of preaching about the kingdom: "Repent (stop conforming to this world and worldly ways by changing the way you think) for the kingdom of heaven is at hand (because I am bringing with me or have already brought a new way for you to think and conform to, and that is the way of the kingdom of heaven)."

Repentance is more than just a religious practice; it is a way of life that is integral to our victory here on earth. When we allow the Word to change the way we think, we position ourselves to grow, be productive, and to be used more effectively by God for His kingdom's purpose.

Confession

After repentance comes confession. From erroneous teachings we have an incorrect interpretation of confession: that it means telling everybody all your business and everything you have done. That is not true. *To confess* comes from the Greek *homologeo* (Strong 3670), which literally means *to speak the same thing*. Other related words and phrases are *to assent with, accord, agree with, declare,* and *admit*. To confess is to recognize that a fact, whether good or bad, has been declared, and to agree that this fact is accurate. Confession is not the act of telling God that we have sinned. He already knows that. When we confess, we agree with God that we have sinned when His Spirit convicts us of wrongdoing. Confession does not involve justifying our actions or behavior or debating or negotiating with Him. He is a holy being; if He declares an action sinful and tells us about it, our only response should be, "Yes Lord, I agree. That was sinful." The Spirit will convict us because His job is to lead us and guide us into all truth. I must stress here that conviction is not the same as condemnation. Condemnation brings feelings of guilt, shame, and unworthiness. Conviction is a gentle nudge indicating that we can do better. Sometimes the enemy can fool us into thinking that condemnation is conviction. We can combat that error by searching the Word for evidence of our conviction. If the Word provides evidence on the matter on which the Spirit convicted you, you're safe. If not, rebuke the condemnation in the name of Jesus, resist the Devil and his advances, and he will flee.

Apply God's Grace

After we have repented and confessed, we have to learn to apply God's grace to our lives to move forward. The application is based on the unlimited and unmerited grace of God and only works only in combination with that grace. We all have reached the realization that, no matter how hard we try, we just cannot live the kingdom life on our own merit. Titus 2:11–12 stresses the power of grace: "For the grace of God that bringeth salvation hath appeared to all men, Teaching us that, denying ungodliness and worldly lusts, we should live soberly, righteously, and godly, in this present world."

In essence, God's grace is expressed when God says, "You cannot live this life without me, so let Me teach you how to do it because I want you to be the best. Let me help you do it and do it right!" Applying God's grace then means that you are taking that statement from God literally and allowing Him the opportunity to help you, lead you, guide you, and train you by the power of His Spirit. God's grace is a manifestation of the power of His Spirit at work in your life. After you have done all the above, you must now apply God's grace to your life to see the growth and the fruit for which you prayed. This is because you receive the promise by God's grace through faith.

Application also involves claiming what is yours. Claiming a promise simply means holding God accountable to His Word. We like to say that God is faithful, but I doubt that we really grasp the gravity of that statement. God is faithful to His own Word. That is why He said, "I watch over My Word to perform it," in Jeremiah 1:12, and, in Isaiah 55:11, "My Word will not return void." God gave us permission to put Him in remembrance of His Word, as it is written in Isaiah 43:26. God is passionate about His Word because, as the King, His Word is His image, and He goes to great lengths to protect the integrity of His Word. So when we seek to apply God's grace in this context, we can visualize a contractual agreement that will be fulfilled.

Let's look at this step in practical terms. Suppose you have been reading the Word (key #1) and you come across Ephesians 4:25, which hones in on the issue of lies: "Wherefore putting away lying, speak every man truth with his neighbor: for we are members one of another."

If you have lied to someone, when you go to pray, the Spirit will bring this verse back to your memory and convict you of lying. That begins the process of repentance. You are presented with the opportunity to change your thinking and your actions regarding lies. Once you have repented, your responsibility now is to agree with the Spirit's conviction. Your reasons for lying do not matter. If the King says that lying is wrong, then it is wrong. Finally, applying God's grace to this scenario involves resting in and allowing God's grace to help you overcome temptations to lie instead of relying on your own strength and ability. This can involve following the promptings of the Spirit when you are tempted to lie. However tempted, then you do not lie because the Spirit will let you know lying is wrong. That response is God in the act of "teaching us to deny ungodliness and worldly lusts" and to "live soberly, righteously, and godly, in this present world."

Following that process of repentance, confession, and application of God's grace puts us on the path to growth, spiritual development, and fruition in the kingdom. The more we practice that process, the more available we become as vessels through which God can work.

Tongues: the secret weapon

The topic of tongues has been the object of debate for centuries. Many books have been written and many messages preached on this subject. Because we don't understand how important this concept of tongues is, we lose out on one of the biggest weapons available to believers. I am not an authority on this very delicate subject, however I still hope that this section can provide some insight on this wonderful and spiritually effective tool.

Some people have many misgivings about the use of tongues. I feel that this use is the most valuable asset that we have concerning spiritual things.

First, what is the concept of tongues? I believe that there are two different types of tongues, natural or earthly tongues and spiritual or heavenly tongues. We must first differentiate between the two. Let us look at natural tongues first. In the passage below, we read that when the Holy Spirit was poured out on that day of Pentecost, all the hundred and twenty disciples who were in the upper room spoke in tongues.

> And when the day of Pentecost had fully come, they were all assembled together in one place, When suddenly there came a sound from heaven like the rushing of a violent tempest blast, and it filled the whole house in which they were sitting. And there

appeared to them tongues resembling fire, which were separated and distributed and which settled on each one of them. And they were all filled (diffused throughout their souls) with the Holy Spirit and began to speak in other (different, foreign) languages (tongues), as the Spirit kept giving them clear and loud expression [in each tongue in appropriate words]. Now there were then residing in Jerusalem Jews, devout and God-fearing men from every country under heaven. And when this sound was heard, the multitude came together and they were astonished and bewildered, because each one heard them [the apostles] speaking in his own [particular] dialect. And they were beside themselves with amazement, saying, Are not all these who are talking Galileans? Then how is it that we hear, each of us, in our own (particular) dialect to which we were born? Parthians and Medes and Elamites and inhabitants of Mesopotamia, Judea and Cappadocia, Pontus and [the province of] Asia, Phrygia and Pamphylia, Egypt and the parts of Libya about Cyrene, and the transient residents from Rome, both Jews and the proselytes [to Judaism from other religions], Cretans and Arabians too—we all hear them speaking in our own native tongues [and telling of] the mighty works of God! And all were beside themselves with amazement and were puzzled and bewildered, saying one to another, What can this mean? But others made a joke of it and derisively said, They are simply drunk and full of sweet [intoxicating] wine.

—Acts 2:1–13 (AB)

In verses 4 and 6, we see that *the tongues* that the disciples spoke were different languages and dialects. Here is where we get valuable insight into the "manifold wisdom of God" (Ephesians 3:10). The Holy Spirit had just been poured out and at that same time it was the Pentecost festival so people from all over the known world at that time were there. Therefore, to spread the gospel of the kingdom with maximal effect, the Holy Spirit gave the disciples the ability to speak in different languages to preach the gospel of the kingdom that resulted in three thousand people getting born again to then go back to their countries to spread what they had heard. Talk about impact!

The spiritual or heavenly tongues, however, are different from known, earthly languages. Consider the apostle Paul's account of speaking in unknown, unearthly tongues.

> True, there is nothing to be gained by it, but [as I am obliged] to boast, I will go on to visions and revelations of the Lord. I know a man in Christ who fourteen years ago—whether in the body or out of the body I do not know, God knows—was caught up to the third heaven. And I know that this man— whether in the body or away from the body I do not know, God knows—Was caught up into paradise, and he heard utterances beyond the power of man to put into words, which man is not permitted to utter.
> —2 Corinthians 12:1–4 (AB)

Many theologians and interpreters of this passage agree that Paul himself was that man who was caught up to the third heaven and that the third heaven was the spiritual heaven where God resides. I believe that this is the heaven that that Paul visited, and I also believe that this incident occurred when Paul was stoned and left for dead outside Lystra in Acts 14. In verse 4, Paul said that while he was in the third heaven, he heard utterances that were beyond the power of man to put into words that men understand. In other words, these heavenly or spiritual utterances could not be translated into any natural or earthly tongue or language. If it was not an earthly language that Paul heard in the third heaven, it was a spiritual language. The spiritual realm is the only other realm that exists; the earthly realm was born from the spiritual realm.

A spiritual tongue is a spiritual language spoken as a result of a believer's personal, spiritual relationship with God. Consider Paul's further testimony on speaking in tongues.

> But as it is written, Eye hath not seen, nor ear heard, neither have entered into the heart of man, the things which God hath prepared for them that love him. But God hath revealed them unto us by his Spirit: for the Spirit searcheth all things, yea, the deep things of God. For what man knoweth the things of a man, save the spirit of man which is in him? even so the things of God knoweth no man, but the Spirit of God. Now we have received, not the spirit of the world, but the spirit which is of God; that we might know the things that are freely given to us of God. Which things also we speak, not in the words which man's wisdom teacheth, but which the Holy Ghost teacheth; comparing spiritual things with spiritual. But the natural man receiveth not the things of the Spirit of

> God: for they are foolishness unto him: neither can
> he know them, because they are spiritually discerned.
>
> —1 Corinthians 2:9–14

This passage shows us that, because we have the same Spirit of God, when we speak in spiritual or heavenly tongues, we speak of matters that the Holy Spirit is teaching us. In other words, the Holy Spirit downloads spiritual mysteries, knowledge, revelations, wisdom, understanding, and application into your spirit. There all these incubate until the appropriate time for them to be used. This is like depositing money in a bank account. The more money we deposit, the bigger the amount grows. The same principle applies in the Spirit. The apostle Jude phrased it like this: "But ye, beloved, building up yourselves on your most holy faith, praying in the Holy Ghost."

Speaking in tongues is supposed to build *you* up. Expression in tongues is supposed to be a private conversation between you and God. Here follows more emphasis on prayer in tongues.

> Likewise the Spirit also helpeth our infirmities: for
> we know not what we should pray for as we ought:
> but the Spirit itself maketh intercession for us with
> groanings which cannot be uttered. And he that
> searcheth the hearts knoweth what is the mind of the
> Spirit, because he maketh intercession for the saints
> according to the will of God.
>
> —Romans 8:26–27

Praying in tongues in our private time builds us up because the Devil can't understand what we are saying. Paul said, in Romans

8, that those who lack the Spirit of God do not belong to God. In 1 Corinthians, he mentioned that the Spirit of God freely gives us all that we need to know. So the Devil cannot understand when we speak in tongues because he does not have the Spirit of God. That is why he is afraid of believers praying in tongues—when we do so, he does not know what to expect.

Paul also wrote at length about tongue-speaking that had gotten out of hand in his first letter to the Corinthians.

> He that speaketh in an unknown tongue edifieth himself; but he that prophesieth edifieth the church. I would that ye all spake with tongues but rather that ye prophesied: for greater is he that prophesieth than he that speaketh with tongues, except he interpret, that the church may receive edifying. Now, brethren, if I come unto you speaking with tongues, what shall I profit you, except I shall speak to you either by revelation, or by knowledge, or by prophesying, or by doctrine?
>
> —1 Corinthians 14:4–6

Paul meant the spiritual or heavenly language that is beyond the power of man to translate into an earthly language. So in layman's terms, Paul meant, "Look, Corinthians, if you all want to talk in spiritual tongues, that is fine. Go ahead and do so. That is not an issue. However, if you are going to speak in spiritual tongues, then do so in your private time because when other people are present, they need to know what you are saying."

In churches today, spiritual tongues are used as a spiritual disguise for people who are empty vessels with nothing to offer. Wanting to appear spiritually sophisticated, these people bring out the tongues. That is incorrect. That is why Paul continued, "I speak in tongues more than all of you, but when I come around you in a group setting, I would rather speak five words that you understand than five hundred words in tongues, which benefit nobody but me. That would be selfish because church is for edifying and encouraging everybody else."

Repentance, confession, and application of God's grace combined with building yourself up in your private time with prayer in spiritual tongues are all essential for the believer who wants to experience substantial growth and productivity. When you speak in tongues, the change will be noticeable—you actually have something worthwhile to say, and you will take the Devil by surprise. He will not know what to expect from you.

Praying without ceasing doesn't mean *always* praying or praying 24/7 all year round. That is obviously impractical. What it means that we should not neglect the opportunities to pray. In other words, pray whenever and wherever you get the opportunity, whether it is a short prayer or a long prayer. Prayer should be more than just an activity; it has to be an integral part of our lifestyle or culture.

Chapter 9

Key #3:
Read Books

The first two keys dealt with the growth and development of the spiritual person within all of us. However, although we are spirit beings, we have a soul that lives in a physical body. The soul is a component that houses the mind, will, emotions, and intellect. At the same rate that your spirit is growing, your soul needs to grow as well. Books or any form of literature can increase knowledge, which is very good. I like the saying that "readers are leaders." It is the truth. The person who reads constantly and expands his or her mental capacity is usually the visionary leader who accomplishes great exploits. The famous American president Abraham Lincoln said it best: "The things I want to know are in books; my best friend is the man who'll get me a book I ain't read."

The ignorance of ignorance

A lot of believers don't progress because they are ignorant. After years of involvement in church, I have concluded that believers are ignorant of ignorance. Permit me to elaborate.

The greatest threat to believers is not sin. God took care of sin through the perfect sacrifice of Jesus the Christ, as related in 1 John 2:2. The greatest threats are not the Devil and his cohorts because they were disarmed when God took care of sin through Jesus Christ, as related in Colossians 2:14–15., Not even we ourselves comprise the greatest of these threats because we have been given back authority and dominion. The Devil was disarmed when God took care of the sin problem through Jesus Christ, as written in John 1:12. If sin, the Devil and his hosts, and even we ourselves are not threats, what is the greatest threat? The answer is very simple, so simple that we often overlook it. The greatest threat to believers is ignorance.

When we are ignorant, we will suffer from all that we don't know. Our enemy, although he is harmless, capitalizes on our ignorance. The Bible constantly stresses knowledge (information), understanding (comprehension of the information), and wisdom (application of the information that you comprehend). Once we become less ignorant through the constant exercise of these capacities, the enemy can no longer victimize or bind us. That is why Paul constantly prayed that the new believers would be filled with revelation and knowledge of God and His Word so that they would not be ignorant of the Devil's tactics, as he wrote in 2 Corinthians 2:11. This same principle also applies to the function and operation of the world system.

Contrary to popular belief, ignorance is not bliss. Ignorance is dangerous. Ignorance places people in bondage and captivity, as the prophet pointed out in Isaiah 5:13, and ultimately destroys them. The opening chapters of Hosea, leading up to chapter 4 and verse 6, provide a picture of what our society looks like today. God said that all these negative developments occurred because of ignorance.

I find it interesting that God says ignorance destroys people and not sin, the Devil, or even themselves. I believe that is because the word *destroy* has to do with purpose. *The Merriam-Webster Dictionary and Thesaurus* definition of destroy is:

- "To put an end to (ruin)"
- "To deprive of life (kill)"

So when you destroy something or someone, you completely ruin it or spoil it, thereby terminating its purpose. Then it cannot function properly or as intended. It becomes good for nothing and ceases to exist.

If you require proof, you need not look far. Just take a look at your own society and community: individuals, families, marriages, businesses, communities, and even churches are being destroyed because of ignorance. Information that these people and organizations lacked might have saved them. Ignorance kept them in mental captivity and bondage and eventually destroyed them. God was very explicit about the consequences of ignorance.

> My people are destroyed for lack of knowledge: because thou hast rejected knowledge, I will also reject thee, that thou shalt be no priest to me: seeing thou hast forgotten the law of thy God, I will also forget thy children.
>
> —Hosea 4:6

God said that the people are being destroyed as a result of a lack of knowledge. Remarkably, He never said that they were ignorant because the knowledge was unavailable. He said they were ignorant because they chose to reject knowledge. Rejection is a willful act; something has to be available in the first place to be rejected. The issue was the willful rejection of available knowledge.

Then God goes on to reject those who have rejected knowledge. This was not because He did not want anything to do with them. Due to their ignorance, He could not use them effectively as priestly vessels. Priests were the mediators between God and the people. They spoke on behalf of God to the people and to God for the people. When people are ignorant of His Word, however, He can't use them to talk (mediate) to other humans about Him.

Then comes what I believe to be the saddest part of the whole verse. This is a principle, so please do not miss it: ignorance is generational, and ignorance is transferable. In other words, if one generation lacks knowledge, their children and grandchildren will also lack it. The ignorant pass down their ignorance and the disorder expands with each generation. Thus each generation seems more ignorant than the previous one, and the trend won't stop. I would venture to say that it can't stop unless we break the prevalent cycle of ignorance.

Destroying ignorance

We saw previously that the concept of destruction includes termination of purpose. When we destroy something, we end its existence by damaging or attacking it to ruin it emotionally or spiritually or to defeat it utterly. So how do we destroy ignorance? Through Proverbs 4:7, the Word says that "wisdom is the principal thing and in all thy getting; get understanding." If we are ever to make the mechanisms of our world function as they were designed and intended to function, we need to know, understand, and apply the principles that govern its existence.

I want to bring your attention to Stephen's discourse on Moses before the chief priest. In Acts 7:22, Stephen described Moses: "And Moses was learned in all the wisdom of the Egyptians, and was mighty in words and in deeds."

Moses, the deliverer, was not an ignorant man. He was well-educated with the knowledge and culture of Egypt, the most advanced society of the civilized world at that time. I believe that Moses was a voracious reader. How else would he have been "mighty in words and in deeds"? Moses was a prince and therefore it is highly likely that he read books on laws, government, and public administration. Although Moses had the knowledge of Egypt, he still needed the wisdom of God to apply and interpret his knowledge correctly as the first administrator of the new nation of Israel. God used the knowledge that Moses gained from his reading as a platform for his growth into Israel's first public administrator.

We also see the Apostle Paul who wrote 13 of the 27 New Testament books and was a brilliant apologist of the Christian faith in his final letter to Timothy, his son in the faith, instructing Timothy on his next visit to bring with him the books and the parchments that Paul left in Troas (2 Timothy 4:13). This indicates that the Apostle Paul was such an avid reader that even in prison he was finding the time to read and gain knowledge. His reading habit is also evidenced in his masterful writing style.

As expressed in Proverbs 10:14 (AB), "Wise men store up knowledge [in mind and heart], but the mouth of the foolish is a present destruction." When we store something up, we save it and put it away for future use. Remember that wisdom is simply the application of knowledge—so how can men apply information that they don't know? Also, how will they know it if it is not stored? How can it be stored by people who never acquired it? It is interesting to note where the knowledge is stored. The verse says it is stored "in mind and heart." In other words, the knowledge you get never leaves you; it is stored in your mind (at the conscious level) and heart (the subconscious level) until retrieved for application as wisdom. Knowledge is a lifetime investment.

I emphasize that we are spirit beings who live and operate in this physical and natural sphere. To operate effectively, we need knowledge of the world. Reading books is part of our process of gaining knowledge and wisdom. However, as kingdom citizens, we have the advantage of the Spirit to provide us with guidance and wisdom, which is simply application of the knowledge that we get from the world, to make the best decisions. Reading books on any topic that can give us advantages in this life is always a plus.

I am quite aware that some religious people do not want to read secular books because they believe that the Bible is sufficient. This kind of thinking is ridiculous and detrimental to growth and development. God speaks through any medium. If He could use a donkey, He could use anything. God gives everybody a different grace or anointing for a particular subject. An expert writing a book on his or her specialty probably has the grace to elucidate that subject for the rest of us.

There is a litmus test for books though. Always measure the subjectivity of a book against the objectivity of the Bible, by which we measure everything. If what you are reading does not align with the Word of God, it may not benefit you.

Benefits of reading

Through my research and experience, I have discovered several benefits of reading.

Cerebral stimulation

Reading provides mental stimulation. The brain is like a muscle, requiring regular exercise to keep it strong, fit, and healthy. Keeping your brain active and engaged keeps it strong. To preserve your brainpower, read and exercise your brain.

Increase in knowledge

Almost everything in life is subject to loss at any time. The only possession that can never be taken from you is knowledge. Why is this important? If you have knowledge, you are in a better position to regain anything else you might lose. That is why people who work to become wealthy and then lose their money are better positioned than persons who get wealth through the lottery or inheritance. The ones who work gain knowledge through work, and that knowledge remains with them. The lottery winners and inheritors never knew how to work. When they lose their wealth, they don't know how to regain it. Whenever you read, you fill your head with new information, and you never know when it might come in handy.

The more knowledge you have, the more equipped you are to tackle any challenge.

Vocabulary expansion

With the current advances in technology, being articulate and well-spoken seems to be a virtue of the past. However, the ability to speak confidently and fluently can be an enormous boost to your self-esteem and a great help in any profession. Reading brings new words into your vocabulary and helps you express yourself accurately. People who are well-read, well-spoken, and knowledgeable on a variety of topics tend to get promotions more quickly and often than those with who lack a high vocabulary and high level of knowledge and awareness. Those who read know more words and are able to communicate their messages clearly.

Improved writing skills

Writing comes right after vocabulary expansion. When your vocabulary improves, so will your ability to write effectively. Reading good writing helps us to write better. A gifted writer is a ravenous reader, and the good effects of reading show in a person's writing. The same way that musicians influence one another, writers profit from the influences and techniques of other writers.

Stronger analytical thinking skills

Reading greatly improves your critical and analytical thinking skills. A keen reader will think about what he or she reads. That reader will analyze and critique ideas and theories to arrive at a logical conclusion. If you have read suspense novels, you may have an idea of what I mean. When I was younger, I used to love *The Hardy Boys* series for that very reason. Many times I solved the mystery before finishing the book. I did not know that I was boosting my analytical and critical skills by noticing and sorting the details of the plot to guess the outcome. When I could not guess the ending, I went back over the plot and used those skills to piece the puzzle together. I put my critical and analytical skills to work in my early reading. As I continue to read, this ability to analyze and critique remains a valuable asset in my work as an adult.

Improved imagination and creativity

Reading good books expands imaginative and creative ability. Books open a whole new world of insight and possibilities. When you read a description, your mind creates it in your head. This is far more dynamic than exposure to the same material through television. You are only limited by what you can envision, and your imagination is limitless.

I would be remiss if I did not mention here that parents should be aware that their children do notice their elders' attitudes toward reading and their reading habits. The more your child sees you reading, the likelier that child is to read as well. The family that reads is a family committed to destroying generational ignorance! We would live in a calmer world if we all allowed ourselves a few minutes a day to focus on a good, life-changing book!

Chapter 10

Key #4:
Monitor Your Associations

Association is powerful. The Word of God is replete with maxims on the influence of the company we keep. Proverbs 27:17 notes, "Iron sharpeneth iron; so a man sharpeneth the countenance of his friend." Proverbs 13:20 pronounces severely on the company we keep: "He that walketh with wise men shall be wise: but a companion of fools shall be destroyed."

We often underestimate the power of other people's influences on our growth and productivity. For growth and maximum productivity, it is imperative that you spend your time with people of purpose and vision. Then you will go in that direction too. People of purpose and vision tend to experience consistent growth and productivity. If you spend time with people who are doing nothing with their lives, it won't be long before you begin to head in that direction with them. You become a product of your social environment. If you are not pleased with yourself or your direction, you must change your social environment—your associates. This principle works in the spiritual sphere as well. If Jesus is truly our friend, the more time we spend with Him, the more we become and act like Him. If that is true, shouldn't the same principle apply to the natural world and our friends and contacts there?

We have to choose consciously to spend our time with people who say, like Paul in 1 Corinthians 11:1, "Be ye followers of me even as I also am of Christ."

Are you spending your time with friends who sharpen your countenance and help you grow and become more like Jesus Christ or with friends who dull your countenance and pull you further away from Jesus Christ? Remember that Jesus is the vine and you are the branches that are supposed to grow and bear fruit. If you are disconnected from the vine, then you will not grow and bear fruit.

First Corinthians 15:33(AB) warns us about negative friendships: "Do not be so deceived and misled! Evil companionships (communion, associations) corrupt and deprave good manners and morals and character."

Whom do you attract? Do you attract people with constructive tendencies, friends who encourage and edify you? Or do you attract people with destructive tendencies, people who discourage you and complain, but never seem to want their complaints resolved? Remember, you are what you attract. Good character attracts good character, and the opposite is also true. It is in your best interest to be around people who are creative, innovative, and able to stretch your mind. The future belongs to those who believe in the beauty of their visions and not in the reality of the present. Your associations play a major role in how you view the future.

Disassociation is sometimes necessary

I am not going to tell you that separating from people is an easy process. That is the hardest thing that anyone has to do, especially when these are people you love. I can tell you, though, that for everything we want to gain, we have to lose something, whether by choice or by force. However, we have to condition ourselves to view every loss as an opportunity to learn and grow despite the pain. Gains and losses represent the changes that provide opportunities for us to grow and mature. If we want to grow, we cannot view change as negative. In other words, no change means no growth. When God wants you to grow, He initiates change by making situations and relationships in your life so uncomfortable that you have no other alternative but to let them go and move on.

I have noticed that many people, especially believers, talk a good talk about the kingdom and purpose. However, very few really understand the concept and the necessity of detachment from hindrances so that they can grow and develop as productive citizens of God's kingdom. Many people view detachment and disassociation negatively. If we detach or disassociate from someone or something for authentic kingdom purposes, the severance is not done out of malice. It is the believer's choice due to internal realization that there is an assignment to fulfill. A sincere desire for growth and productivity will always require a disassociation or detachment by either will or force.

You don't have to look very far for examples. I have often noted that celebrities make comments such as, "If you want to get somewhere, you have to leave some friends and acquaintances behind and connect with people who are like-minded and have similar goals." One used a travel analogy: "Not everybody can accompany you on your journey; you have to know the difference." Another said, "You have to accept the reality that most people will not understand your passion or purpose." Yet another, commenting on Facebook, stressed the importance of positive companions: "You need to associate with people that inspire you, people that challenge you to raise higher, people that make you better. Don't waste your valuable time with people that are not adding to your growth. Your destiny is too important."

Those who are left behind, even if they supported the believer's endeavors, may resent being left behind. I have observed that no one has a problem with separation until he or she is left behind.

The abandonment of some friendships and associations is a natural process. The more your life begins to align with your purpose, the clearer your vision becomes. The clearer your vision becomes, the more focused your priorities become, and the more you focus on what God has called you to do. Then growth begins. Once that progression begins, not everybody can accompany you to your destination. Even Jesus said to the Jews, "You cannot come where I am going," in John 8:21. Sometimes we may have to tell some of our associates, "Sorry, friend, I know where I am going. As you are right now, you cannot accompany me where I am going."

When you speak like that, you will offend some people but let me assure you that you are not doing anything offensive. You are identifying and eliminating distractions because growth and productivity in God's kingdom demands it, as expressed in Luke 9:62. God Himself provides the right connections to encourage and assist you in your growth and development. If God could add people to the newly formed church in Acts daily, then He can certainly add people to your life to help you grow, mature, bear fruit, and become productive.

People who grow and are fruitful have invariably disconnected themselves from those who stifled their growth, whether intentionally or not. People like Abraham and Paul had to leave certain people to fulfill God's purpose. Attached to that purpose is growth and maturity—these men's faith grew exponentially when they left the social environments that had stifled them. Jesus' disciples had to change their associations to be with Him for three and a half years. As a result of that change, the good news of the kingdom spread throughout the world and brought substantial growth to the worldwide church!

Misconceptions about disassociation

A common misconception is that disassociation means resentment or rejection of those left behind. It does not. It simply means that you realize that there is more to gain from life, and some associates cannot take you to that next level. When Paul recognized that he and Barnabas had two different visions, he realized that they should separate, as is written in Acts 15:38–40.

Another misconception is that disassociation means that you have forgotten your roots. Dropping former friends does not mean that you have forgotten where you came from. Outgrowing our surroundings does not mean that we have forgotten where we came from. I did not forget where I came from; I remember that very clearly. The difference is that I cannot stay there because, like Jesus, I know where I am going, as written in John 8:14. As with Joseph, Esther, and Moses, we will eventually have to separate ourselves from some of our associates so that we can rescue them later on.

When the call for growth, maturity, productivity, and bearing fruit comes, believers will have to separate from some friends to move onward and upward. That's the juncture where the rubber meets the road. Be prepared for ridicule and slander. If you fulfill the mandate to bear fruit, you will be slandered, ridiculed, and accused of ingratitude by those you have left behind. Do not worry about this. Remember, persons only throw stones at fruitful trees, not barren ones. The mere fact the stones are being thrown at you figuratively speaking means that there is some fruit on you that they would like to have. Your responsibility is to keep growing and producing the fruit. You are not the first to experience it and most certainly won't be the last. It is all part of the process.

Many people are comfortable in their present condition. That is fine. Some people are perfectly contented when doing the same things and going the same places year after year. It is important that you do not force them to see where you are going. Most likely, they will not understand, and they will probably resent you all the more for disrupting their comfort zone. However, if you want to move onward and upward, that is fine also. If you want to move upward and onward and be fruitful in the kingdom of God, you have to be consistent, determined, and disciplined in your choice of friends and associates. If you want to achieve the greatness within you, that is the path that you must take.

Perhaps you are comfortable as you are but have an issue with people who have left you behind so they can be productive. If so, that is wrong—those people are acting appropriately to achieve their goals. Rather than getting upset, maybe you should take a look at where you are now and where you are going. Perhaps, then, you will see why they separated from you.

When God calls for purpose, growth, and higher productivity, believers *must* leave negative associates behind. Sadly, many people know about purpose, growth, and productivity but very few understand their dynamics, and even fewer apply them. Let me encourage you to be among the few who apply the principle of association. Power lies in application. Your growth depends on it.

Chapter 11

Key #5:
Find a Mentor

T his last key is indubitably one of the greatest investments you can make for growth, development, and productivity. Usually, a mentor concentrates on one aspect of a mentee's development; however a good mentor will be committed to your holistic development. As a mentee, you submit yourself to the counsel, instruction, and correction of your mentor, preferably an older and wiser person. Your mentor should already be at the level where you desire to be. Alternatively, your mentor may not be at that level yet but is nearer to it than you are. It is common sense that the mentor and mentee should have the same goal. For example, if my goal is to purchase or build a house, it would be silly of me to ask advice from someone who is still paying rent and has made no effort to buy or build.

Mentoring is so important that the Bible abounds with examples of mentor/mentee relationships. Several mentor/mentee relationships the Bible mentions are those between Paul and Timothy, Ruth and Naomi, Moses and Joshua, David and Solomon, Mordecai and Esther, Elijah and Elisha, and Jesus and the disciples. Careful observation of the dynamics of these relationships reveals that the persons who were mentored experienced significant growth and were even more productive than the persons who mentored them. That is the power of a good mentor. Interactions with your mentor should challenge and encourage you to develop spiritually. In doing so, you will become a sharper thinker and more productive kingdom citizen, even to the point where you might outperform your mentor.

During my research and from my own experience, I have discovered four attributes to seek in a mentor, a leader you can emulate. These criteria can be found in 1 Timothy 3:1–13, Titus 1:5–9, and Titus 2:2. Although these are the stated qualifications for a bishop, elder, or deacon, they can be applied to mentors too. Persons in these positions should be able to become mentors also. These areas are as follows.

- spiritual life
- family life
- professional life
- social life

Let us examine these four areas in greater detail.

Spiritual life (Titus 1:7, 9 and 1 Timothy 3:6)

The spiritual life of a mentor should be noteworthy. Paul says, in the book of Titus, that the mentor should realize that he is a "steward of God." This means that mentors know they are managers and that everything under their auspices was given them by God to manage and develop. Your mentor should view you as a person to guide toward full potential, not a subordinate to control. This is an important fact. Mentors are never to control you. Only a mentor who understands the mentorial role as manager or caretaker of the mentee God entrusted to him or her will know that.

Mentors must also be wholeheartedly committed to the faith and able to use the Word to teach, encourage, exhort, comfort, correct, and refute those who oppose the truth. The mentor must do this with conviction and through love. That approach helps the mentee because it provides those teachable moments when the best learning takes place. A lesson after the fact is less effective than a lesson right when the best opportunity presents itself.

Spiritually, mentors must have experience in the faith and not be novices, as the Bible says. A novice lacks the significant experiences in the faith that teach people about the complexity of life. Also, if they are given the opportunity to mentor someone while still fresh from their salvation and redemption experience, novices may develop a sense of pride and superiority. That can only lead to a destructive end and casualties in their wake.

Family life (1 Timothy 3:2, 4–5 and Titus 1:6)

The family life of the mentor should be stable and exemplary. A married mentor should be in a faithful and committed relationship to one spouse. A mentor cannot teach you to be consistent, faithful, and unwavering and to display unconditional love if the mentor doesn't do exactly that.

Next, regarding family life, is the conduct of the prospective mentor's spouse and children, if any. Is the spouse an asset or a liability to the mentor? Does the spouse's behavior detract from or improve the mentor's life? A negative spouse may be symptomatic of a deeper issue problem. Are the mentor's children well-behaved or loose in morals or conduct? Do they reflect the attitudes and character of the mentor, or are they unruly and disorderly?

To paraphrase Timothy and Titus, if a mentor's house is out of order, that person cannot teach anything of significance; that person cannot even teach those in his or her own house.

Professional life (1 Timothy 3:7)

A mentor should be able to provide an example in professional life as well. Mentors should demonstrate excellent qualities and sound, ethical business practices. They must understand and value work and transmit that word ethic to their students. They should advance in their careers or businesses through honorable methods that are worthy of respect and emulation. Mentors should not be lovers of money, ready to obtain it by questionable or dishonest means. If the desire for wealth overpowers the ability to exercise sound reason and judgment, they will resort to dishonest practices, which will soon catch up with them.

Social life (1 Timothy 3:2, 8 and Titus 1:7, 2:2)

In social settings, mentors should display pristine character. Here are a few desirable traits that 1 Timothy 3 and Titus 1 (AB) mention.

- above shame
- circumspect or prudent
- temperate
- self-controlled

- sensible
- well–behaved
- dignified
- disciplined
- hospitable
- not controlled by alcohol
- non-confrontational
- gentle, considerate

- pacifistic
- patient, peaceable
- not self–willed
- not arrogant
- lover of that which is good (people or things)
- upright
- fair-minded

When the mentor demonstrates positive behavior to the mentee, the mentee then imitates that behavior. This emulation shows the power of positive associations. People become like those with whom they spend their time. In this case, the mentee becomes like the mentor in all four aspects.

So, when seeking a mentor, it is important to exercise due diligence. First Timothy 3:10 (AB) says that deacons and, by extension, mentors should first be "tried and investigated and proved, then if they turn out to be above reproach, let them serve." Choose a mentor who can offer what you seek. Once you are satisfied, you can choose that person as your mentor.

Mentors need not be perfect unless your definition of *perfect* is what the Bible calls *perfect*. The biblical definition of *perfection* is *maturity*. Mentees need mature mentors so they can learn to grow and become mature as well. If you decide to become a mentee of a matured mentor, you will be amazed at how your life will expand by leaps and bounds as you develop into a mature, productive, and fruitful citizen of the kingdom.

As Paul explained to the Roman believers, such growth starts only when we are transformed by the renewal of our minds via the Word of God. Growth indicates that maturity is occurring. With maturity comes the fruit manifested in the lives of believers to the ultimate glory of God and His kingdom, of which we partake.

Believers should not aspire only to be born again and wait until heaven calls them home. Their goal should be productive growth—bearing lasting fruit that transcends generations. If you do not believe that is possible, how then do you think that we got the Word of God in the form of the Bible that many of us hold so dear? The writers of the various books of the Bible, under the inspiration of the Holy Spirit produced those fruits (books) that we have today centuries ago.

That is also how the late Dr. Myles Munroe is able to transcend generations because he produced over sixty books that will outlast him. The late André Crouch did the same thing with his music – transcended generations. What is even more important than that is the fact that their remaining fruit, even in their death, is still giving God glory. It doesn't get any better than that! What will be your lasting fruit? Will it be books? Will it be an album of songs? Will it be a business? Will it be an enterprise? Will it be a ministry? Will it be churches around the world? Will it be a law that is so impactful that it bears your name? Will it be an invention that can change the world? I am convinced that all of these and more is possible to them that believe that it is possible.

Believers, God has called you to bear lasting, remaining fruit so that ultimately when men see what you have produced, they will glorify your Father in heaven and the kingdom that you are a part of. Therefore, by the authority of the Word of God and with the blessings of God I charge you to go forth, be fruitful and multiply what you have been given for the Kingdom of God! In Jesus' name, amen!

Bibliography

Bible Study Tools. Galatians 5:22-23 KJV. 2014. 22 October 2014 <http://www.biblestudytools.com/kjv/galatians/passage/?q=galatians+5:22-23>.

Earl Radmacher, Ronald B. Allen, H. Wayne House. New Illustrated Bible Commentary. Nashville: Thomas Nelson, 1999.

King James Version/Amplified Bible Parallel Edition. Grand Rapids: Zondervan, 1995.

Merriam-Webster. Merriam-Webster's Dictionary and Thesaurus. Springfield: Merriam-Webster Inc., 2006.

Munroe, Myles. Releasing Your Potential. Shippensburg: Destiny Image Publishers, 1992.

Online Etymology Dictionary. Identity Definition. 2001-2015. 30 April 2012 <http://www.etymonline.com/index.php?term=identity&allowed_in_frame=0>.

Renner, Rick. Sparkling Gems from the Greek. Tulsa: Teach All Nations, 2003.

Strong, James. <u>Strong's Complete Word Study Concordance.</u> Chattanooga: AMG Publishers, 2004.

Wikipedia. <u>Fruit of the Spirit.</u> 30 March 2015. 20 April 2015 <http://en.wikipedia.org/wiki/Fruit_of_the_Holy_Spirit>.

William Edway Vine, Merrill F. Unger, William White Jr. <u>Vine's Complete Expository Dictionary of Old and New Testament Words.</u> Nashville: Thomas Nelson, 1984.

Zodhiates, Spiros. <u>The Complete Word Study Dictionary New Testement.</u> Chattanooga: AMG Publishers, 1992.

Appendix

About Visionary Leadership Ministries International (VLMI)

Visionary Leadership Ministries International (VLMI) is the international ministry of Darren Wilson, dedicated to helping the kingdom of heaven advance and expand in the earth by **inspiring**, **empowering**, and **transforming** lives from the inside out.

The problem

The moral and ethical fiber of Saint Martin, the Caribbean region, and the world is unraveling at an alarming rate. Among the causes are poor self-images, family disintegration, crime, unproductiveness, poor leadership in business and government, and countless others. Such problems are infiltrating and destroying our countries. Countless people have proposed solutions to address these issues, but they constantly fail. They do not provide real, long-term answers. This is because many of the proposed solutions address these issues as short-term issues, not as the ongoing problems they are. If we continue to address these issues from a short-term perspective, the results will almost inevitably be the same. We need long-term proposals to begin to address these long-term issues.

The philosophy

Darren Wilson and Visionary Leadership Ministries International believe that, by teaching the Word of God, we can inspire people to structure their lives under the kingdom of God and empower them with the tools necessary to live successfully and purposefully on earth. Then they can use their learning to transform society—individuals, families, churches, businesses, and communities—with the abundant kingdom lifestyle.

The vision and purpose

What is our vision, our purpose? Our goal is to see believers display their kingdom purpose, mature, and live the kingdom lifestyle abundantly in every facet of spiritual and natural life. VLMI believes that when people begin to recognize their kingdom purpose, grow into it, and live free of the bondage of religion, they begin to walk freely in the kingdom's authority. That authority is given to them by God through Jesus Christ as kingdom citizens. Then they will have a positive impact on human society through the kingdom lifestyle.

Contact information

For speaking or ministry engagements or more information on VLMI, contact
Visionary Leadership Ministries International
vlministries.sxm@gmail.com
darren_wilson38@yahoo.com
Facebook page: Visionary Leadership Ministries International

Printed in the United States
By Bookmasters